Jessi-Cat

Jessi-Cat

The Cat That Unlocked a Boy's Heart

Jayne Dillon
with Alison Maloney

W F HOWES LTD

This large print edition published in 2014 by
W F Howes Ltd
Unit 4, Rearsby Business Park, Gaddesby Lane,
Rearsby, Leicester LE7 4YH

1 3 5 7 9 10 8 6 4 2

First published in the United Kingdom in 2013
by Michael O'Mara Books Limited

A CIP catalogue record for this book is available
from the British Library

ISBN 978 1 47125 074 3

Typeset by Palimpsest Book Production Limited,
Falkirk, Stirlingshire
Printed and bound by
CPI Group (UK) Ltd, Croydon, CR0 4YY

MIX
Paper from
responsible sources
FSC
www.fsc.org   FSC® C013604

For my Dad, who would have loved this book. Also, for my family, cats and anyone with an invisible disability.

CONTENTS

WHAT IS SELECTIVE MUTISM?

Selective Mutism is an anxiety disorder of childhood in which affected children speak fluently in some situations but remain silent in others. The condition is known to begin early in life and can be transitory, such as on starting school or on being admitted to hospital, but in rare cases it can persist right through a child's school life.

These children usually do not talk to their teachers and may also be silent with their peers, although they do communicate non-verbally. Other combinations of nonspeaking can also occur, affecting specific members of the child's family. Often the child has no other identifiable problems and converses freely at home or with close friends. He/she usually makes age-appropriate progress at school in areas where speaking is not required.

The essential feature of Selective Mutism is the persistent failure to speak in specific social situations (e.g. at school, with peers and/or the teacher), despite being able to speak in other, more familiar situations.

Children with Selective Mutism are likely to . . .

- Find it difficult to look at you when they are anxious – they may turn their heads away and seem to ignore you. You might think that they are being unfriendly, but they are not – they are just not able to respond.
- Not smile, or look blank or expressionless when anxious – in school, they will be feeling anxious most of the time and this is why it is hard for them to smile, laugh or show their true feelings.
- Move stiffly or awkwardly when anxious, or if they think that they are being watched.
- Find it incredibly difficult to answer the register, or to say hello, goodbye or thank-you – this can seem rude or hurtful, but it is not intentional.
- Be slow to respond – in any way – to a question.
- Become more anxious when under pressure to speak.
- Worry more than other people.
- Be emotionally sensitive.
- Be physically sensitive e.g. to noise, smells, touch, crowds.
- Be very sensitive to the reactions of others – they may misinterpret these reactions.

• Find it difficult to express their own
  feelings – because it is painful to do so.

From SMIRA (Selective Mutism
Information & Research Association),
www.selectivemutism.co.uk

PROLOGUE

ABOUT A CAT

Lorcan stood at the front of the class, as thirty eager little faces gazed back at him from their desks. Beside him, on a table, sat a box containing a fluffy little miracle, the very reason he could face this momentous task. At the age of eight, he was about to make his first public speech and the subject he'd chosen was his beloved pet, our beautiful Birman, Jessi-cat.

Before Jessi came into our lives two years ago, speaking in public wouldn't just have been daunting: it would have been impossible. Lorcan suffers from selective mutism, a debilitating anxiety disorder, which prevented him from speaking to classmates and teachers and struck him dumb for the best part of his early school years. Since the arrival of Jess, he has come on in leaps and bounds and, in December 2012, when it came to his turn in the Hot Spot – where the children do a short talk on something they are interested in – Lorcan's teacher asked him if he wanted to do it. To her surprise and mine, he said he did.

It was only natural that Lorcan decided to do the talk on Jessi-cat, so we checked with the teacher that she would be allowed into school, and she agreed. We opted to keep the speech simple and have lots of things to show. Lorcan chose what he wanted to include and we noted down a few sentences about the charity Cats Protection's Cat of the Year Awards, which Jess had won in the summer. Lorcan prepared well and, on the morning of the Hot Spot, he seemed fine. He went into school as usual, taking along his bag of cat-related items, and I went home to get Jessi. When we arrived at school, she was lying on a comfy blanket in her cat carrier and seemed quite relaxed, so I handed her over to the teacher and waited, anxiously, in the reception area.

We knew it could go one of two ways: Lorcan could find his confidence and do it really well, or struggle and clam up. Fortunately, his best friend had offered to help with the presentation, so I comforted myself with the thought that, if he struggled, George would help him. As Lorcan had been making huge progress with his talking at school, I was desperate for his big moment to go really well.

After a nail-biting ten minutes, my heart leaped as Lorcan came through the door. Then relief flooded over me as I saw the huge grin on his face. When he had been sent back to the class, the teacher told me Lorcan had done a brilliant job.

He had not needed George's help and had even answered questions asked by the children, who loved having the cat in school. He had talked about the awards she had won and shown them various mementoes, including the programme from the National Cat Awards ceremony at the Savoy hotel, a cat toy of Jess's and the beautiful pictures Simon Tofield, the creator of the British animated series Simon's Cat, had kindly drawn for him. The teacher showed me a picture of Lorcan addressing the class and was delighted that he'd overcome this hurdle, as was I. To stand up in front of a class of around thirty children and to be the focus of attention was a huge achievement for Lorcan.

Feeling elated, and a little choked up, I took Jess home and couldn't wait to share the news with friends and relatives. On my Facebook page, I posted:

> Lorcan took Jessi-cat into school today and did a talk on her in front of the whole class! He talked about the National Cat Awards and answered questions. I don't believe he would've been able to do it by himself without the cat there. She is a precious blessing, living up to her fancy [pedigree] name of Bluegenes Angel.

Everyone was thrilled, and I was flooded with supportive messages from loved ones, who have followed his struggle with selective mutism. They understood what a huge event this was for all of us. And for me and the family it was another reason to be thankful that this gorgeous cat came into our lives. She has been a true Angel.

CHAPTER 1

A NEW BEGINNING

A few weeks before Christmas 2003 I took my two-year-old, Luke, to a birthday party for a boy the same age. As the children played, having plenty of noisy fun, I chatted to a friend who was pregnant, and due to give birth any time, and another expectant mum. In the midst of all the baby talk, I suddenly started to feel really strange, but I soon put it out of my mind as the frantic festive preparations took over.

That year, as in most years, we planned a quiet family Christmas at home, with me, my husband David, our two sons Adam and Luke, and my mum Pauline, who lives just around the corner from us in Manchester. At some point in the festivities I began to feel odd again, and I said to David, who happens to be a GP, 'I'm pregnant. I'm sure I'm pregnant.'

'Don't be daft,' he responded with a laugh. 'You always think you're pregnant.' We hadn't been trying for a baby, and he was convinced it was just my imagination, but I wasn't so sure.

On Boxing Day, I popped out to the sales at the Trafford Centre – the huge shopping Mecca, which is dangerously close to our house – and I picked out loads of lovely bargains. As I queued at the cash desk and paid for the mounds of new clothes, I remember thinking, This is probably really silly because I'm not going to fit into them in a few months.

When I got home, I collared David again.

'I'm pregnant,' I said. 'I'm definitely pregnant. I can't explain it but I just know I am.' To shut me up, rather than because he believed me, David went straight out to buy a pregnancy test kit.

I shut myself in the bathroom to do the test and the thin blue line soon confirmed what I already knew. I didn't say anything. I just showed David the positive test and he said, 'Oh, so you are.' It was never planned, but it was a lovely surprise, and we were both delighted.

My oldest, Adam, had come along before I met David and was now sixteen, and Luke was two, so another baby would complete the family perfectly.

As soon as I knew baby number three was on the way, I thought, What shall we call this child? My husband's Irish and I thought of loads of girls' names, but when it came to boys' names I was stumped, so I instantly started looking at names. When I was pregnant with Luke we'd chosen George, but he didn't suit George, so we settled on Luke instead. This time I fancied something a bit different. I trawled through Internet sites of baby names and kept coming back to Lorcan, and it just stuck. It means 'fiery warrior'.

At twenty weeks we went for the routine scan and I told the sonographer I didn't want to know what sex the baby was. She didn't tell us but, even though she quickly moved the ultrasound on, we could both see it was a boy. For a midwife and a doctor, it's not hard to spot!

I had spent three years training as a midwife after my first baby, Adam, was born. I found it a hugely rewarding and deeply satisfying job, and I loved the fact that I helped bring all those babies into the world.

Before Luke came along I had been working at the maternity unit at Trafford General, just around the corner from our current home, but, by the time I had Lorcan, I had cut back and cut back on my hours and I was working only about one night a week. Even so, my past work and my familiarity with the unit meant Lorcan's birth was a very laid-back affair. Labour was very fast. After the first pain I was on the phone telling the midwives I was on my way in, and he was delivered by my close friend, Natalie Webb-Riley, and everything went really smoothly.

Lorcan looked a bit shocked after the birth – maybe the speed of it all proved a bit alarming – but his face soon relaxed and he turned into a very pretty baby. Dave was at the delivery and we both held him as soon as he was born. We had to wait for the paediatrician to examine him before I could leave, so Dave nipped home to get Luke, so he could meet his new brother. I could hear Luke long before I could see him as he ran down the hospital corridor yelling, 'Mummy, mummy!' at the top of his voice. I'm sure the other patients were thrilled.

Luke glanced at the baby but was more interested in my nightdress because it had a picture of Betty Boop on the front! We had bought a present, as if from the baby, for Luke so he didn't feel left out. It was a Peter Pan action figure he wanted.

I was in hospital only a few hours. As a midwife, I knew I was fine, knew what to look out for, and I didn't want the other midwives running around after me. Believe me, they have enough to do. They didn't even give me a bed because, although I was tired, it seemed that everything had gone swimmingly, Lorcan was a healthy weight – at 7 pounds 10 ounces – and I was ready to go home.

When I brought him home from the hospital, Luke still wasn't awfully impressed. He had a quick look at his little brother but soon decided he wasn't interested. Adam had been through it once before, so a newborn baby held no fascination for him either.

My mum came to see us as soon as we got home, as I was already up and about and feeling fine. Later in the week, my brother came with his children and then we quickly settled into a routine and carried on.

Lorcan was a lovely baby, but he cried a lot, which frightened Luke. For a tiny bundle he was very vocal and, whenever he started wailing, Luke would sit with his fingers in his ears to drown it out. On one occasion it got so much for him he even asked me, 'Can we take the baby back?'

Night-times were a nightmare. Luke had been a textbook baby. We put him in his cot and he went to sleep, but Lorcan was a lot harder to cope with. He was very cute, and very good during the day, but during the night he was a horror.

When Luke was a baby, David had to get up early to travel a fair distance to work, so he would feed him before he went. But having two young children is a balancing act and, once we had Lorcan, he did more with Luke, who was now three, while I took care of the baby. He still had to be up early for work, so he learned to sleep through a lot of crying.

By contrast, Lorcan was pretty placid during the day, especially if we were out. Mum and I would often take him to the Trafford Centre, when it was raining, because it was a great way of getting out and you can still walk the pram about. When Luke was tiny, he was hideous on shopping trips. He wanted everything, he was always throwing tantrums and we were constantly carrying him out of shops, screaming. Lorcan, on the other hand, was great. As a toddler, he would even help us shop. My mum would say, 'Could you help me choose?' and he'd point at things from his pram. We could spend all day wandering around boring clothes shops, and he would sit and smile, without making a peep.

Once the baby could walk and crawl about, Luke showed a bit more interest and would get down on the floor to play with him, which was a relief. I had been worried that Luke would never really like the baby. The first time Luke showed a real interest was when we had just had the garage on the side of the house converted into a playroom. Lorcan was about seven months old and Luke came home from nursery to find the new playroom carpeted and decorated.

'Can I play in the playroom? With Lorcan?' he said.

I was delighted, as this was really the first time he had wanted to be involved with the baby. He also got quite protective. One day, when Lorcan was about eight months old and Luke was about four, I took them to a soft play centre in the local area. They were sitting together in a ball pit when a little girl touched Lorcan with her toe by accident, very lightly. He wasn't hurt and didn't even cry, but Luke wasn't having that. He looked very cross and told the poor little girl, in no uncertain terms, 'You just kicked my baby!' He has looked after his little brother ever since, in lots of different ways.

Trafford General maternity unit – which has sadly been shut down since Lorcan was born – has played a huge part in our lives. As well as being Lorcan's birthplace it is also where David and I first met, in 2000. There was no lightning bolt from the blue – in fact I can't even remember our first meeting – and my first words to him were probably, 'Could you sign this prescription?' Or 'Can you come and check a patient?'

But we were working side by side at a clinic every week and we got on well.

David and some of the other doctors were on a six-month rotation and, when their time was up, there was a big leaving party for all of them. It was a really great night and we were getting on like a house on fire. At the end of the evening, because he lived in the hospital and I lived round the corner, we ended up going home together and our relationship escalated from there. We started seeing each other more and more after that. He wasn't really what I thought of as my type, to be honest, but we got on incredibly well and something just clicked. Very early in the relationship, we just knew that we would be together.

I had had Adam when I was twenty, and I'd scraped by as a single mum for twelve years before David came along. It wasn't always perfect, but I lived with my mum and dad and they were always there to support me. I would not have managed to do my midwifery training or hold down a job with shifts if it hadn't been for them. Midwifery is unpredictable and, if the woman you are looking after delivers around shift finish, you won't finish at the expected time, so it is crucial to have good childcare. I also worked full-time nights as much as possible, which meant more time with Adam during the day. I had the use of my mum's car and no childcare worries, so it was a perfect arrangement. My dad sadly died when Adam was five and, with my mum widowed at such a young age, we were company for her as well.

Adam was a really well-behaved boy. Although he wasn't diagnosed until he was eighteen, he was suffering from Asperger's syndrome, and that often makes children better behaved than normal, because they like to follow rules.

David got on with Adam from the start. Adam was about twelve when they met but he has always been very easygoing and quiet, so he's no trouble to anyone, and that made it easier for the pair of them to get on.

I nearly died from shock when I found out I was pregnant with Luke. We really hadn't been together very long and we certainly hadn't planned kids at that point. I'd been feeling really sick and unwell and, by now, Dave and I had a really close relationship, so I just told him I thought I was pregnant. He has always wanted a family, so, as soon as I told him that, he said he hoped I was. We bought a test kit and, when it came back positive, he couldn't stop smiling.

I was more apprehensive – not about the baby but about the labour. Like many women I'd had a horrible time with my first labour and delivery and as a midwife I'd seen many more women go through some awful births. I'd also had a big gap between pregnancies and was anxious in case there were problems. But David was thrilled and very excited, so I put my fears to one side. By this time we were in our thirties and, although I had one child, and would quite happily have left it at one, any baby is a little blessing. Once you have them, planned or not, they're brilliant, they are your baby and you love them absolutely.

When I was three months pregnant we rented a bungalow near to my mum's house. Dave had changed jobs by then and was working quite far away, so could only spend weekends off at home.

Luke was born in 2001, in May. His birth was easy and he was a dream baby, the kind that all mums would love to have. He smiled at three weeks, sat up before he should, and did everything a little bit earlier than he was expected too.

Neither of us is very conventional, or into

tradition, so I didn't feel the need to have a ring on my finger, even with the imminent arrival of Luke. But we did get engaged while I was pregnant and, in 2003, finally tied the knot, mainly because our parents kept asking us when we would. There was no romantic proposal, just a joint decision to make it legal, and we definitely didn't want a big expensive wedding.

On the first sunny day of the year, in March, we went to the register office in Sale, Trafford, with my friend and her husband and our children, and then came back home and had a few friends and family round. Dave wore a suit he already had and my wedding dress was an impulse buy from some time before. We had already decided we would get married and had not got round to doing anything about it but, while Mum and I were browsing in the shops on one of our regular shopping trips, I spotted a beautiful knee-length silk dress in dark pink. My mum said it would make a lovely wedding dress – a hint that didn't go unnoticed – so we bought it. Then Dave and I decided to get on with it, so I rang the register office, we took the next available date they could offer and we were sorted. All very practical – but that's the way we are.

The ceremony was very memorable because we chose the shortest one possible and because Luke, who was fifteen months old, spent the time charging up and down the register office, then tried to open the fire door at the back of the room. On the way home we called at a local pub,

Jackson's Boat in Sale, for a celebratory drink with Julie and Kieran, our witnesses, and their little boy Daniel, who is a few months older than Luke. After one drink we were asked if we would leave, as the babies were laughing too much and disturbing the patrons! It was probably just as well, as everyone was waiting for us back home and Mum and Auntie Vera had been slaving away to prepare a fabulous buffet.

It was all unplanned and very last-minute, but it was great. Unfortunately, Dave's family live in Ireland and couldn't get flights over at such short notice but we had a really relaxed afternoon with friends and neighbours. I still have my wedding dress hanging upstairs – complete with a fetching wine stain down the front!

CHAPTER 2

LORCAN, LILY AND LAUGHTER

Lorcan was born on 12 September 2004, the day that Luke was due to start nursery school. The nursery is attached to the local school, Woodhouse Primary, so their new intakes work around the school year, but they kindly put Luke's start date off for a couple of weeks, because of our new arrival. When the agreed day came, I left the baby with my mum so I could take Luke on his own, and we walked the short distance to the school together. Naturally, Luke was nervous at first and held my hand for a second but, when he saw all the other kids playing, he was absolutely fine. He couldn't wait to join in and he was soon sitting on the floor, playing with cars and Duplo blocks, which are a construction toy like Lego, but with bigger pieces.

Luke attended nursery for only two and a half hours a day, sometimes in the morning, sometimes in the afternoon, so it was difficult to go out. I would either have to be there to collect him at 11.30 a.m. or have him ready for the afternoon sessions at 1 p.m., as well as looking after a new baby. But it was great that Luke settled well, especially as he'd had to deal with a new baby at home.

My mum is retired and lives just around the corner near the nursery school entrance, so we spent a lot of time with her. I would often leave the baby at my mum's house while I picked Luke up from nursery on his own. We'd then all go back there for lunch.

I was still working for about one night a week and some extra shifts when the maternity unit were short-staffed, so my mum would babysit if Dave was at work. The rest of the time, with Luke at nursery, I was at home with Lorcan, but he was hardly any bother during the day, as long as he was out and about. He was a very placid baby, happy to sit in his buggy for hours. We went to Wales one weekend and while Luke played on the beach for a couple of hours, building sandcastles and paddling in the sea, Lorcan would sit in his buggy and watch the world go by. He didn't once scream to be lifted out.

But the bad nights carried on. Lorcan never slept through as a baby – he barely does that now. He was a struggle to get to sleep and then he would wake up and scream through the night because he absolutely hated the cot. When he was ten months old, I tried putting him in the room with Luke, who was on one of those raised beds with ladders and chests of drawers underneath. A few days later, I walked into the room in the morning and Lorcan was climbing up the stairs to Luke's bed! I flew across and grabbed him, just in time. After that we had him in our bed for a while, which was far from ideal. He was a little bit better in a bed but he was always a hideous sleeper.

When he was a small baby I taught Lorcan baby signing. There were no classes near me at that time so I bought a book and got him to sign a few basics to use. He picked it up really quickly and it was a real lifesaver, because he could tell me when he was tired or hungry and let me know when he needed milk.

Lorcan spoke very early. I don't remember his first clear word but it was the usual thing – starting with ba-ba, da-da, ma-ma. It was just sounds and experiments and nothing unusual, pretty normal speech. By two he was chatting away in proper sentences, almost on a level with his brother, who was three years older. Once, he answered the phone to Natalie, the midwife who delivered him, and when he handed it over she said, 'Was that Luke?' I told her it was Lorcan, and she was quite excited because he had such beautiful speech, and so early.

When Lorcan was one and a half my mum

accidentally shut the car door on his index finger, and the tip of it was crushed. My poor mum was so distraught that she couldn't even come with us to the hospital. As you can imagine, I was pretty distraught as well, because he was so young. We rushed to Accident and Emergency at Trafford General and, when we got there, the nurse asked me for his date of birth. I was in such a state I couldn't remember, and all I could do was sob, 'Oh my God, I don't know.'

It was just the tip, and it turned out nothing was badly broken, so it could have been a lot worse, but poor Lorcan was clearly in pain and yelling at the top of his lungs, which made the long wait in the crowded waiting room even more excruciating. Eventually, we were ushered in for an X-ray and he was still screaming blue murder. Then we went in to see the doctor and, weirdly, the moment she produced the X-ray, Lorcan shut up to have a look. Up to that point the whole blooming hospital – and probably half of Manchester – could hear him and, as soon as he saw the image of his hand on the light box, he was transfixed. I was so relieved – mainly because he was going to be OK, but also because the noise had finally stopped!

Lorcan was a sweet-looking baby, so, whenever we went out shopping, or David took him over to the newsagent to get his paper, adults would smile at him and make a fuss. But, if anybody spoke to him, he'd hide behind the counter. At home with the family, he was a real chatterbox and loved learning new words, and when he was one and two, I considered it to be perfectly normal to be shy and hide from strangers. We didn't think anything of it – just the usual toddler reaction to faces he didn't know. Looking back now, I guess there must have been other signs in his early years, but when they're that young it doesn't register as unusual behaviour.

The thing is, Lorcan was never shy in the usual sense. He'd happily throw something at a stranger or grin at them and, even at that young age, he wouldn't do the classic hiding in the clothes or behind my legs. He just blanked people. Whenever anybody spoke to him he would stare back at them and would never reply.

When Lorcan was around eighteen months old, he was a little chatterbox. One lunchtime, Dave dropped me and Natalie off at the Trafford Centre, where we were meeting some midwife friends for lunch. Lorcan chattered away nonstop from our house to Natalie's and as soon as my friend got in the car he clammed up. He sat in his car seat and didn't say a word.

That may not be unusual in a toddler. What was probably more unusual was that it wasn't just adults. The silent treatment extended to kids as well.

On one occasion, when Lorcan was two, my Aunt Vera came to visit my mum, and she brought her grandson, Jacob, who is a very similar age to

Lorcan. My mum was used to Lorcan chatting merrily away and thought these two would get on like a house on fire, so she had Lorcan while I was sleeping off a night shift at home. He was there for two hours – not a word. He spoke beautifully at home but, in that couple of hours, Jacob was chatting away and playing the whole time – and my son didn't utter a thing. Again, we just thought it was normal for children to be a little shy or quiet in certain situations, especially before they go to school or nursery. As a mum, you don't think anything of it. It is only when it continues that it becomes a problem.

On Luke's birthday, in May 2007, we had a Mad Science party at home with around nine boys from school, most of whom Lorcan was familiar with. The party organizer showed the boys various scientific experiments and let them take part in some, and they had a wonderful time. But I remember being very puzzled because Lorcan refused to join in and, again, didn't utter a word throughout the party.

A few months later, shortly after he turned three, we were in the local Early Learning Centre on a Tuesday, when they would get lots of the toys out for children to play with. Suddenly, a small boy about Lorcan's age just appeared around a corner and Lorcan jumped out of his skin and ran back a few steps, which struck me as odd.

When he thinks it's just us around him, Lorcan

is a noisy, vivacious and mischievous little chap and always has been. When he was two, we took the whole family to Disneyland in Paris for a treat. Lorcan screamed for the entire fifty-minute flight, but when we arrived at the airport, somewhat frazzled, he was fine.

While we waited for our luggage, I took him round the corner to use his portable potty – a plastic contraption with a plastic bag inside for easy disposal in a bin. After he had been, I fastened up the bag of wee and asked him to hold it for a couple of seconds while I put the potty away in the bag. The little horror calmly took it from me and placed it on the luggage carousel then watched it glide away with some delight. I asked him what he'd done with it and he happily pointed, smiling sweetly all the time. I had to jog alongside and retrieve it, hiding my embarrassment from my fellow passengers.

The gift shop in our hotel was packed with Disney merchandise and Lorcan loved it all, so we forked out for a huge pen to keep him happy. As he came out of the shop, he did a little jig and started singing, 'This is my big pen' at the top of his voice. He thought we were the only ones there. He didn't realize he was being watched by a big crowd of about twenty, who burst into delighted laughter!

As anyone who has been to Disneyland knows, the famous characters – Mickey Mouse, Minnie, Pluto, Goofy and the like – don't wander around only in the theme parks themselves, but are frequently seen in the hotels and surrounding spaces. The kids flock to have their pictures taken with them and Luke was up for a picture every time, but Lorcan wouldn't go anywhere near them. He wasn't scared by them, just refused to go close enough to have a picture taken. While we were having a meal, he was quite happy for them to come up to him, but if they were standing, beckoning him over, he wasn't having any of it. Then again, we tell kids not to talk to strangers, so that's perfectly normal.

In May 2006, the whole family went to Ireland to visit David's family, and attend his Aunt Caela's wedding. Dave's mum and dad and sister Stephanie had visited us shortly after Lorcan was born but most of the family hadn't met Lorcan, who was only eighteen months old. We filed into the church for the ceremony and we were ushered into the second row, but Lorcan was in a very mischievous mood. He kept running up and climbing on the altar and we kept getting up and dragging him back to the seat, where he'd squirm until he got free again.

It was a beautiful service and a friend of the bride, who had a really lovely voice, had been asked to sing. She'd barely reached the chorus of her melodic performance when Lorcan launched into a loud high-pitched version of his own wedding anthem. A church full of wedding guests sniggered behind their hymn sheets as Lorcan got louder and louder, really getting into the swing of things, but Dave and I were mortified.

Eventually it got too much, so Dave took him outside and was swiftly followed by Luke. But the pair of them were now in the mood for mischief. There was an awkward moment when some people came to the graveyard to lay flowers, only to find Luke and Lorcan literally dancing on some of the graves. Needless to say, we beat a fast retreat to the hotel.

The following morning Dave was walking down to breakfast with Lorcan, when he noticed a card hanging on a bedroom door which said, 'Do not disturb'.

'What's that?' he asked. Dave explained that they didn't want anyone to disturb them, probably because they were still asleep. Lorcan looked up at Dave, grinning, banged on the door and set off running up the corridor, swiftly followed by his embarrassed dad.

As we were going home on the ferry, Lorcan started screaming at the top of his lungs. He didn't seem to like the noise of the engines and nothing we could do would calm him down. The screaming was getting seriously loud and was disturbing other people, so we were obviously embarrassed that we couldn't quieten him down. In desperation I ran into the gift shop to get something to distract him. A small furry monkey caught my eye. I paid for it quickly while listening to the ear-piercing screams from Lorcan. I handed it to him and he was immediately quiet. Relief all round!

Lorcan loves monkeys. He has lots of them in his bedroom and often sets them up around his bed when he's getting ready to go to sleep.

'They're there to protect me,' he says.

'From what, Lorcan?' I asked him once, but he couldn't explain.

We've always had pets in the family and, when the younger kids were born, we had a cat called Flo, but she was well into her adulthood and didn't do much. Although the kids loved her, she didn't hold much interest for them and she was quite old, about eight or nine, when Lorcan was born. She had got used to living in a reasonably quiet home, with me, David and Adam.

Once the two boys were old enough to start playing, and were running around and screaming, she spent a lot of time upstairs!

When Lorcan was three we decided to get a dog, mainly for Adam's sake. He had finally been diagnosed with Asperger's syndrome and was going through a rough time generally. We'd heard and read a lot about animals and dogs and how they can help people with the condition, so I started looking into it. I'd never had a dog before and I didn't know anything about them. I started looking at different breeds and I kept coming back to Tibetan Terriers, but I was not one hundred per cent sure. Then, as luck would have it, we were walking in a local park one day and we saw a gorgeous little puppy there, white with brown patches. I said to the owner, 'What breed is she?'

'She's a Tibetan Terrier,' she replied. I was hooked.

We looked everywhere and I struggled to find a female, which we wanted – mainly because we'd already chosen the name Lily after Lily Potter in the Harry Potter books! I also wanted white. There are black and sandy-coloured coats too, but I much preferred the white. I spent hours on the Internet and ringing around, and there were lots of male dogs, and black dogs, but the only white female we could find was two hundred miles away in Dagenham. Undeterred, we drove all the way down to pick her up and it took us four hours, but we weren't disappointed. When we got there we were faced with the sweetest little white puppy, and we totally fell in love. The decision was made and we brought her straight home.

All the boys took to her, instantly, and she was very, very cute. Lorcan adored her but was rough with her from the start, in a playful way. Luckily, she proved to be an extremely tolerant dog. He would get her in a headlock and drag her about, play tug-of-war and chase her about the house. He never hurt her but he has always played pretty rough.

Because Lily has a top coat and an undercoat, grooming is very important to avoid tangles and matting, so she goes to a local dog-grooming firm, where she is seen by a lovely lady called Gill. She has a spruce-up every eight weeks and she is always a little reluctant to go through the door, and I think that is because she doesn't like me to leave her rather than her not wanting a bath. But, as she is a family pet and a really messy dog, she really needs regular baths. It costs quite a lot, depending how matted her fur is, but it's worth every penny. I do bath Lily at home when she gets really mucky, but she never ends up looking as beautiful as she does after a visit to the groomer.

On one occasion, when Lorcan was five, I had just brought Lily home from her grooming session, and she looked beautifully white and clean. In fact, she was so white Lorcan must have decided she was a blank canvas, because the next thing I knew he had drawn three lovely lilac pink stripes along her side in felt pen. Lily, being the placid pet she is, sat still all the while, letting him do it. I didn't actually see him drawing on her but I had a pretty good idea who was responsible and, when I quizzed him about it, he just giggled mischievously. We got some really funny looks, and a few comments, when I took Lily out for a walk but people who know us as a family didn't need to ask whose handiwork it was. Luckily, it wore off after a few days.

When the children were little, they had all the vaccinations they were supposed to have, despite the MMR scare. This, you may remember, was the controversy surrounding the combined measles, mumps and rubella (or MMR) vaccination after a medical paper in the *Lancet* medical journal in February 1998 suggested it could cause autism. That research paper has since been discredited.

We weighed up the risks and looked at the studies and we personally felt that we'd rather have our children vaccinated than risk the diseases. Both Adam and Lorcan showed traits of Asperger's syndrome as tiny babies, before the jabs. Whatever problems he has were there from the start, I'm quite sure of that.

Lorcan's favourite book, when he was tiny, was *Kisses Are Yuk!* by Julia Jarman. It's a really funny picture book about a little boy called Jack, who hates cuddles and kisses, and it's no wonder he identified with that. From a very young age, Lorcan hated to be touched or cuddled. If I said to Luke, 'Can I have a cuddle?' he would say, 'Course you can.' We don't cuddle much now, because he's a bit older, but he would still cuddle me if I asked him to.

With Lorcan that was never an option. Occasionally, if he was upset, or Luke was mean to him, or he'd hurt himself, I could sneak a hug and he would stick with me for a while, but he didn't like it and still doesn't. Even now, I sneak a kiss when he's asleep sometimes but I would never try when he's awake because I know it would upset him. I wouldn't grab him and kiss him during the day, even in a playful way, because that would distress him – way beyond the usual jokey thing between a mother and a son, who might just say 'Aw, get off, Mum!'

He particularly hated his neck being touched and the skin there seems incredibly oversensitive. Even when he was little, he always had to wash his own neck and I wouldn't dry it, because that would send him loopy.

Because Lorcan was never a good sleeper, even as a toddler, we got into a routine after Luke started school and was learning to read. Dave bathed the boys, then I would read with Luke while he would put Lorcan to bed. He wouldn't go to sleep without someone in the room with him so Dave would stay with Lorcan until he dropped off, just sitting or lying on his bed. Sometimes, Lorcan would hold David round the neck, to make sure he didn't leave, and he'd fall asleep with his arm there, so Dave got a lot of hugs – by default. We never left Lorcan to cry at bedtime. Some children are genuinely scared and I think it is very damaging to leave them to cry. We don't know why he was scared at night as a tiny boy, and he couldn't tell us.

Even Nana got an unexpected close encounter with Lorcan one night, when we were out at a Christmas bash. She wasn't very familiar with his bedtime routine, so she tucked him in and said goodnight. As she turned to leave the room, he pulled the duvet back and patted the bed invitingly, smiling endearingly at her. She soon realized that he was used to one of us lying with him. She had to lie there until he was asleep, then my poor mum found she couldn't get up. In the end she had to roll off the bed onto the floor to extricate herself.

While they are not hugs and kisses, such moments of intimacy become more important when a child is uncomfortable with most physical contact.

In one respect, I was lucky that I had been through all this before. Not liking to be touched or cuddled is a common trait in many – but by no means all – children on the autistic scale and Adam had never really liked being hugged, either.

With Lorcan, any display of affection was rejected. If I said, 'I love you', there was no reaction, nothing at all. But, because I'd been through it before, it didn't upset me as much as it might. If I hadn't already done it, I know I'd be thinking,

He doesn't like me. Why doesn't he love me? That would be a natural reaction. I'm sure many mums think, What have I done? and wonder if they didn't bond with their baby properly. If I didn't know that Lorcan really does love me, I might be in pieces. It may look as if he's being cold and not bothered, but I know that's not true.

Dave took it all in his stride, too. He is very mild-mannered and never forces it, but he'll say something like, 'Lorcan, come and have a look at this picture in the paper,' and Lorcan will sit next to us. Or if we're reading he often plonks himself down on the sofa with us. He's not cuddly and, even when he was younger, he wouldn't come and sit on our laps, but he will sit with us, and that gives us that sweet sense of closeness.

Of course, there were moments when I longed for him to come and cuddle me, or tell me he loves me. That would be lovely, but he's not going to do it and that's just the way it is.

CHAPTER 3

NURSERY NERVES

Four months after Lorcan's third birthday, in January 2008, he started at Woodhouse nursery, the same one Luke had attended before going up into Reception class. Lorcan was very familiar with the building, the teachers and the other children because he was used to coming with me every day to drop Luke off and pick him up. From a very early age I had got him out of his pram and let him play on the floor, or he would be picked up by the teachers, so he got used to the nursery environment and it wouldn't be such a shock when it was time for him to go there.

Because of the familiarity, and because at home he was such a boisterous and outgoing child, I thought he'd settle better than Luke, who was a much quieter boy. But I couldn't have been more wrong.

To start with we eased him in gently. First we had a visit during which I stayed with him, and he was fine; he sat there quite happily. But when I tried to leave him, even for a short while, he really wasn't happy. He screamed his head off.

32

Thinking this was perfectly normal at first, and that he would calm down after I'd gone, I reluctantly pulled away and left him there. In the first few weeks he was doing only half-days, instead of a full session, so I figured he would settle in.

After a couple of days, however, the teaching assistant, Mrs Gayner, pulled me aside.

'He's refusing to take his hat and coat off,' she said. 'He wouldn't even take his mittens off, for the whole session.'

We all realized straightaway that this was his way of objecting to my leaving him, and I was obviously distressed, because my other two hadn't reacted like that. Luke had been a bit anxious and had grabbed my hand as we went in, but he soon dropped it and went off to play. But, when you have a child who's screaming at the top of his lungs every time you drop him off, as heart-wrenching as that is, there's not a lot you can do. I was shocked and very concerned, and it took all my strength and resolve to leave him there every day, but I knew the staff at the nursery well and I knew they'd tell me if there was a problem. I also knew it would be wrong to take him out of nursery. I trusted the staff because they're brilliant and you just have to get over it, whatever happens.

At that age, they have to go to nursery because the alternative is sending them off to school a year and half later, having had them at home full-time, which would be an even bigger shock. Nursery is a great way of getting used to going somewhere every day and mixing with other children, learning social interaction and how to behave in a learning environment.

'What are we going to do?' I asked Mrs Fannon, the teacher. I didn't have a clue how to handle the situation but I was hoping that, as a nursery teacher, she would have the answers. I was right to put my faith in her, she and the nursery staff were all brilliant. They worked out a plan whereby I stayed for a while, then I left him for twenty minutes at a time, and we built it up gradually. It took weeks and weeks but it worked and he was doing full days at the end of it.

Lorcan was one of the older ones in the year group, so he was given a full eighteen months of nursery before starting school. That way he had more time to deal with the trauma of starting in a new environment, before going into Reception class.

The phasing-in period took a few weeks, which was fine for me because I didn't work, but, if I had been a mum who needed to go back to work and had relied on those hours at nursery, it would have been a nightmare. Once we'd cracked it, he went happily every day and looked forward to playing with the other children. He loved school. To this day, he's never refused to go.

A few months after Lorcan settled in, I went to pick him up as usual and Mrs Fannon collared me and asked if she could have a quiet word with me. She sat me down and said, 'We're really worried because Lorcan isn't speaking.' Wow! That didn't sound like my noisy little terror. She also told me she had noticed the little smile that Lorcan glued onto his face when he was anxious, so I knew she had been paying close attention to him.

'He said the odd word to start with, in answer to direct questions,' she explained. 'Then he got quieter and quieter and then he just stopped speaking altogether. We can't get anything out of him at all.'

As soon as she had finished, I jumped in and said, 'Do you think it could be selective mutism?' I have no idea where that thought came from, but I must have read about it somewhere without even knowing that I was taking it in. It hadn't occurred to me before that point that anything was seriously wrong. I just thought he wasn't happy to leave me.

Mrs Fannon looked relieved at my reaction. The staff had looked into the condition before talking to me about it and she had printed out a leaflet to give to me, but I think they were worried at how I would react, perhaps thinking that I would become hysterical or just refuse to believe there was anything wrong with him. Nursery carers must see all sorts of reactions from parents when they raise an issue, but I tend to have a very practical view to any problem presented to me, so I was quite calm. I thought, Right. We've got a problem. Let's get on and deal with it.

It made it easier that the staff and I all thought it was the same thing. Once we all agreed it was selective mutism, we could move forward.

As soon as I got home from the nursery, I rolled up my sleeves and jumped into action. As it was all new to me, I got onto the computer and started looking for more information. I found the Selective Mutism Information and Research Association (SMIRA) website (smira.org.uk), which was really informative and also includes a forum so you can read of other people's experiences and get advice. Apart from being a brilliant source of information, it somehow helps to know you're not alone, that other people have been through the same.

For those who are unfamiliar with selective mutism – which is the vast majority of people – it is an anxiety disorder in which sufferers speak fluently in some situations but are completely silent in others. According to SMIRA it affects six in every thousand children, around the same as classic autism, yet, as I was soon to discover, very few doctors or paediatricians are trained in dealing with it, if they've heard of it at all.

I didn't want to bother Dave at work, so I waited

until he got home to tell him what Mrs Fannon had said. As he's a GP, I asked him if he'd had any training in that field, or whether he knew something about it. He'd never even heard of it, which is probably true of most GPs, and yet, if you have a problem like this, your doctor would be the first place you'd go. Unless they have experiences of it themselves they don't know anything about it, and therefore will not be able to spot it. In some cases, I've heard that parents are told, 'They'll grow out of it.' But in most cases that's not the case. It can get worse as they get older if nothing is done about it early on. There are adults with selective mutism who are unable to speak in certain situations and, obviously, that is a truly debilitating condition in adulthood.

The nursery had suggested that our first port of call should be an appointment with the local speech-therapy department and they told me they would request it and that I should also request it as a parent. I applied, and a few weeks later I received a letter saying that we would have an appointment within eighteen weeks of the date of our request. It was far too long to wait, with Lorcan so close to starting school and not even coping with nursery, and I was not happy. All the research I had read said that early intervention is crucial, so I didn't want to hang about.

Determined to speed things up, I rang the speech-therapy centre and said, 'Can we go private?' I was prepared to pay £400 as a one-off, just to get in there and get some help.

The lady on the other end covered up the phone with her hand and, in a stage whisper, said, 'This woman is asking if she can go private. No?' Then she came back and told me, 'No, sorry, you can't.'

'The child can't speak! He's at school, and he can't tell anybody if he's hurt. He can't tell anybody if he needs a wee. He can't tell anybody if he gets punched or someone's mean to him. How is that not urgent?' I fumed. At that point I was getting really upset, mainly through frustration. I could cope with the fact that he had a problem, but we needed to deal with it.

Fortunately, we were given an appointment soon after that. Within a few weeks, we finally got to see a speech therapist – only to find that she had never dealt with this problem before, which was a big hurdle. She knew the theory, and she was a really nice woman, but she had no experience in this field, so the school were just left to deal with it.

Like all the people who first meet Lorcan, the speech therapist tried to talk to him. Walking into one of these medical meetings for the first time can be daunting, and you often feel that you're being judged as a parent. You can almost see them thinking, What are you like at home? Are you an overanxious mother? A smotherer? Or cold?

You feel as if they're trying to catch you out sometimes. As time went on, each new expert would try to talk to Lorcan, and I'd say, 'Go for it.' But he would always blank them. Sometimes he'd smile, depending on whether he liked them or not, but he never spoke.

The speech therapist did some nonvocal assessments on him, getting him to point to the answers to questions, and he scored really high on that. Sadly, that is not much help, either, because often people think, Oh well, he's clever. He'll speak when he's ready.

This is often the case with children with selective mutism, because they tend to keep up fairly well academically. If you have a 'shy' child who sits at the back of a class or nursery, does their work and doesn't cause any trouble at all, what do you do about it? In most cases, nothing. It's all too easy to assume that everything is fine.

That's one problem. Another is that some people seemed to think he was being stubborn. I can understand that. I have even thought that myself on occasion, at the beginning, wondering if he was doing it on purpose, but you can't keep that up, day in and day out, when you're doing a full day of school. It would just be impossible, no matter how stubborn you are.

Anyway, after her initial tests we didn't get a formal diagnosis but the speech therapist agreed with us, and the nursery, that Lorcan was suffering from selective mutism.

By this time, I had strong suspicions that Lorcan was also on the autistic scale, so I raised this with her.

'I have an older son with autism and I believe Lorcan might have it too,' I said. She did a few more tests and told me they didn't see any signs.

'Do you not?' I said. 'Well I do.' A mother just knows.

Anyway, the speech therapist gave the nursery a programme, called 'Breaking Down the Barriers', to help Lorcan, but the trouble was that she had never come across it before and had no knowledge of how to implement it properly. She literally read it to the nursery teachers from a sheet she'd printed off and she couldn't sit there and talk about it or answer questions, because she had no experience of it.

Before we were given the programme, we had initially done all the things that you shouldn't do to get him to talk at nursery, like bribing him with sweets and toys, asking him why he couldn't speak and whether anything was wrong. But, once we realized he wasn't controlling it, and he was physically unable to speak, we obviously stopped that, because it really wasn't helping.

Asking him why he couldn't speak at school was a waste of time, because he just couldn't explain. One time, when I tried to get it out of him, he just pointed to his throat, which seemed to back up the theory that selective mutism is as physical as it is mental, that it is just impossible for a person with selective mutism to speak in certain situations.

Also, as it's an anxiety disorder, constant questions can be counterproductive, putting the child under more pressure and therefore causing added anxiety.

The nursery staff were truly wonderful. They made him an IEP – Individual Education Plan – setting out what they were going to do and what were all the right things: not making him speak, not bribing him, trying to encourage him to laugh and join in. The treatment is basically designed to take the pressure off him, let him know that he doesn't have to speak if he doesn't want to, and then they came up with a very intensive programme, which is play-based to start.

Basically, a carer works on a one-to-one basis with the child and gets him to establish a bit of a relationship and have fun. Then they start using musical instruments, just making a noise, so they blow into a recorder or bash a drum. Then they make animal noises and it goes on from there. It sounds like something anyone can do but it is hard, and the school did struggle because, after the initial contact, they got no more support from the speech-therapy department.

There were just two staff in the nursery – the teacher, Mrs Fannon, and the teaching assistant Mrs Gayner, whom Lorcan used to follow round like a little shadow. The nursery is very close to the house, so I would often walk past with the dog when the children were playing outside and I would peep over the fence to see what the kids were up to. I always knew where Lorcan would be: holding Mrs Gayner's hand.

As the teacher, Mrs Fannon had to teach the whole class but, when the other children were playing outside, Mrs Gayner would often take Lorcan inside and get the musical instruments out, or play a little game with him. She worked really hard with him for three sessions a week. After a while they brought another child in, then another, to encourage him to speak to a few more people, and eventually another adult, a teacher. It seems bizarre and it's very long-winded but it did work.

One of the things we had in the nursery was a talking book, which allowed us to record ten seconds of audio at a time. So at home we would draw pictures of something, then he would speak about it to the talking book, then he would take it into school and let Mrs Gayner listen to it. He didn't mind that and, at the beginning, it was a useful tool to let her hear his voice. I would often wish, as we sat chatting as a family, that everyone else could see how vocal and boisterous he was at home, but it was only we, and my mum, who saw the real Lorcan.

At Christmas, all the children took part in the nursery Nativity play and Lorcan was to be one of the three kings. The nursery supplied the costume, so there was no need for me to whip up a tunic and headdress for the occasion.

As they were so young, it was all very low-key, just a cute little show for parents and grandparents. At first, I was worried he would be given lines, or would be the only one who couldn't speak, but not many of them had words to say and, of those who did, lots of them got things wrong, as you'd expect.

Of course, Lorcan was one of those who didn't have to speak – and he wouldn't have done anyway – but he was very good and did everything he was supposed to, laying his precious gift by the crib. He looked very happy and seemed to enjoy every minute.

At the age of three, Lorcan adored *High School Musical.* He used to watch the films over and over and would copy all the dance moves – as long as nobody was looking. He also knew all the words to the songs sung by Zac Efron's character, Troy, and sang them endlessly at the top of his voice. He was less keen on the female characters!

Because we wanted the nursery to see him as he was at home, we even made a DVD of him singing the songs, just to prove that he could speak and sing. Lorcan agreed to let the class watch the video and, although he would never have spoken or sung in front of them in that way, he smiled happily as they all watched it.

The nursery programme worked well. He started off just answering the odd word and made slow but steady progress throughout the year.

After Lorcan had been on the programme for a few months, Mrs Fannon announced she was pregnant. That was a terrible blow for us, as she'd been so supportive, and I panicked about who would cover her maternity leave and the impact this would have on Lorcan. I spoke to one of the school governors who would be interviewing the prospective teacher and I even went as far as accosting an ex-teacher from the school at the swimming baths and trying to persuade her to take the job!

When I discovered that Mrs Fannon's replacement was a man, I wasn't sure what to expect. But when he arrived my fears soon vanished. Mr Mottershead was absolutely brilliant. He was really good with Lorcan, and all the kids. With the naughty ones he was a lot more firm. He wouldn't stand for any nonsense, but he was fun at the same time. He called the kids 'mate' and would get down on the floor to play, and Lorcan actually spoke to him.

In the summer term, Lorcan's last at nursery before going up to school, Lorcan made huge progress. He was smiling and talking to Mr Mottershead on a daily basis and we were thrilled. He had even made some real friends, which I was really chuffed about.

There was one little girl who was Lorcan's life-saver. Ella was the daughter of a friend of mine, someone I used to work with, and she was a cute little kid, full of confidence and very chatty. She really took to Lorcan and she used to drag him around to play with her and yak away at him, and she didn't seem to care that she got little vocal response. Ella came home with us once or twice and she was lifeline to him; she was lovely.

But by the end of nursery there was also a really nice set of boys that he played with on a regular basis, and who seemed unfazed by Lorcan's quirks. Then he found one in particular, George, who became his best friend and has helped him an awful lot ever since. George instinctively understood that Lorcan couldn't speak in certain situations, and began speaking for him. It was a relationship that would last him well into primary school, and is still thriving today.

By the time he left nursery, Lorcan was talking aloud a lot more. He still didn't speak directly to many people, but he would play with them and he would join in with the staff during activities, and his speech was getting more normal. Even though he didn't necessarily speak directly to his classmates, he would answer if he was spoken to by a member of staff, especially Mr Mottershead. At the end of the day he would say, 'Bye, Lorcan' and Lorcan would shout, 'Bye' at the top of his voice. We were finally getting somewhere.

Oddly enough, I then started to worry about the opposite problem. I suddenly thought, What if he starts being the same at school as he is at home? because he can be quite wild and rowdy. So I thought I'd end up being called in to the nursery for different reasons altogether. The nursery even had to tell him to be quiet a couple of times, because he was being a bit too loud.

As the term drew to a close, I went to an open day at the nursery. To my amazement and utter joy, Lorcan was speaking. He wasn't speaking just to people he knew, whom he spoke to directly: he was shouting out in front of other parents, which David and I thought was brilliant. He just talked in a really loud voice and most of the parents didn't know about his selective mutism so wouldn't have thought anything of it.

It was just a normal lad being loud as far as they were concerned, but I was bursting with pride. I was so happy that day and full of optimism. I actually thought, Brilliant! We're sorted. It was a huge breakthrough and a sign that he was really beginning to progress – and his nursery teachers thought so too. A report from the nursery, in June, stated,

In the past two weeks Lorcan has begun to speak to his friends and peers during play in both the indoor and outdoor classroom. At times, this can be frequent and fluent sentences, especially when unaware of direct adult presence.

Lorcan has made fantastic progress this term, with his verbal communication confidence, due to his recent breakthrough, and is now showing improvement on a weekly basis. He has reached and exceeded his targets this term and we hope this will continue for the rest of the school year and into reception.

Then he moved up a class . . .

CHAPTER 4

SILENT SCHOOL DAYS

During the summer holidays, everything was very different from the way it had been at school. Lorcan was like he always is, a normal chatty little boy, at home, at least. And he still had a wicked sense of humour.

One day in August, Dave was downstairs pottering about when he heard cries from the upstairs toilet. Lorcan was shouting, 'Dad, Dad, come and save the day! Lorcan's wasting all the toilet roll! *Dad, Dad! Save the day!*' As he shouted, he was whizzing the toilet roll holder round and round so the paper was flying all over the floor. Little menace!

At home, with us, Lorcan's selective mutism is rarely evident but there have been occasions when he goes silent on us. One night, when he was four, I woke to find him at the side of my bed. This was nothing unusual as he rarely stayed asleep all night and often came to find me on a night prowl. What was unusual was that he was scowling and did not speak. I asked him if he was OK and he didn't reply. Assuming there must be something wrong, I started going through a list.

'Are you hot?' I asked. No reponse.

'Are you thirsty?' No response.

'Cold? Frightened? Have you had a nightmare?' Nothing. He just stood there, scowling and not looking at me.

'Do you have a headache?' I eventually asked. His only response was a very tiny flicker of the eyes. I gave him some Calpol, which he took willingly enough, and put him back to bed and he was fine. The next morning he was back to his old self.

Apart from that one occasion, he has never been completely silent with us, but I have noticed that he tends to stop speaking when he is poorly.

That summer, I had some Air Miles accumulated, so we decided to book a holiday. I didn't have enough to fly very far, which was fine because we are not huge sun worshippers and we like to have plenty to do when we go away, so it had to be somewhere that was good for sightseeing and activity. Luke and Lorcan both have a real interest in World War Two, so we decided to go to Guernsey, as it was occupied by the Germans during the war and I thought that would fascinate them.

We stayed in a lovely hotel right on the beach

and had a really busy five days. There were castles to see, beaches to play on, and museums to visit and everywhere we went there was a lot of information about World War Two for the boys to get their teeth into.

One morning we were in the dining room of the hotel eating breakfast, and it was very early, so we were alone. Lorcan was eating his croissant, dabbing his mouth demurely with his napkin, when he declared, 'I'm as posh as a pig!' We all laughed so, inevitably, he kept repeating it, ad nauseam. We were the only people in the dining room, so he was happy to babble away, but he did stop talking when the waitress came into the room.

Lorcan was in his element in Guernsey. The boys really enjoyed sword fighting along the battlements of castles. We went to see all the lookout towers dotted around the island, where they could look through telescopes, which was wonderful, and there were the many museums where Lorcan was interested in seeing the weaponry and other items.

One day, we visited the German underground hospital, which had taken three years to build and was used for only three months, to house German soldiers injured in the D-Day battles. It's the biggest construction in the Channel Islands and the huge stone corridors stretch for miles. I found it a bit creepy and couldn't wait to get above ground, but Lorcan loved it. There were huge guns the boys could mess with and old telephones they could play with. As usual, Lorcan spoke to us if nobody was there but as soon as other sightseers appeared he fell silent, or whispered if he needed to tell us something.

The weather was perfect, lovely and sunny with a cooling breeze. Lorcan loved playing on the beach and finding little fish and sea creatures in the rock pools. It was a wonderful holiday and we came away with some really lovely family memories.

Later in the holidays, we took the kids over to Ireland to see David's family, and to attend his sister Marie Louise's wedding. The wedding was at a beautiful hotel near Ashford Castle, on the borders of County Mayo and Galway, and the boys had a wonderful time exploring the castle grounds. During the ceremony, Lorcan and I sat at the back, away from the rest of the family, as I expected him to start fidgeting and become meddlesome but he surprised me by being quite good. He just scooted along the pew a few times and then sat smiling – although he did let out an audible gasp when his dad got up to give a reading!

Dave's side are a big Irish family, so, whenever we are there, there are a lot of people about. Lorcan didn't speak to any of them for the whole time we were there but, again, it's not uncommon for a small child to be shy or silent in those circumstances. Unlike the last time, we now knew about the selective mutism and had told them as soon as we found out, so they knew what to expect and everyone was very accepting. Both our families have been very supportive.

I explained to Dave's family that, if they wanted to ask him a question, it was best to phrase it so that he could answer it with a nod or shake of the head, and they all did that very well. By this time, Luke had also become a great help, and quite protective of his little brother. He would often jump in and answer for Lorcan, not deliberately, perhaps, but he had become quite used to speaking for him, so it was a natural reaction.

For example, if Dave's mum asked, 'What do you want for your tea?' Luke might say, 'He likes beans on toast.' One of his uncles asked Lorcan if he wanted to go outside to play football. Lorcan looked at Luke to supply his answer and then trotted outside happily when Luke said he would come too. He has always been really good with Lorcan and he puts up with a lot. Lorcan is either hugging him or battering him senseless but his big brother has had his back since he was a baby. He's also a really good role model, because Lorcan can look up to him and see how he behaves, and Luke teaches him things and explains things very patiently to him. Without Luke, I think he would have struggled more, even at school.

In September 2009, after a lovely summer break, it was time to start in Reception class. At the end of the summer holiday, Lorcan and I went to visit the Reception classroom and met his new teacher, Mrs Mellor. She showed us round the room and we took a video of it, so Lorcan could see it again at home, as we thought that would help to familiarize him. Then Mrs Mellor asked what Lorcan was interested in but, of course, he didn't answer. I told her about his love of soldiers and history and she kindly set up a little area with toy soldiers for Lorcan to play with, which he really enjoyed.

The nursery school is actually in the school, so, effectively, all the little ones have to do when they reach Reception age is move into a different class-room. That's why both the children went there, because I thought it would be less unsettling for them if, once they got used to nursery, they stayed on the same premises when they went to school.

Lorcan knew all the staff, and the nursery children even sit in assembly sometimes, so it was a perfect situation.

The older children from the nursery moved to the next class and the younger ones stayed behind. There were a few children who joined the school who hadn't been at the nursery, so the dynamics of the group changed slightly, but he was very familiar with both the Reception teacher and the teaching assistant, so we hoped the move would have minimum impact.

Even so, the speech therapist had warned us he would regress, just because of the change in situation, so we had anticipated a small setback. In October 2008 I had received a letter mentioning the possibility of a backward step the following year, when he started school but, amazingly, it also said that Lorcan was going to be discharged from the books. After coming up with a sketchy programme and not following it through, it was thought that no more needed to be done, just months before he actually went to primary school.

I stood in the hall, open-mouthed in disbelief, as I read,

> Lorcan is making excellent improvements in his willingness to talk to others and has worked well with his teaching assistant through the 'Breaking Down the Barriers' programme. We have discussed the possibility that Lorcan might suffer a slight relapse in September but Mum and school staff are well equipped to deal with this should it arise. I am therefore discharging Lorcan.

It was to be the first in a long line of health bodies washing their hands of the problem, and hoping it would go away. In the summer, before Lorcan went to school, he was once more assessed by the speech-and-language therapist, as I had fought to get him back on the books, and she judged that his speech had improved and discharged him again. By the end of Reception we had been seen and discharged twice. They did some nonverbal assessments and decided they didn't see any signs of autism, so dismissed us.

On Lorcan's first day of school we were given a particular time to turn up. This was so all the children didn't arrive together. The staff could then settle each child in individually. We got him dressed in his brand-new uniform – navy jumper, white shirt and school tie with long grey trousers. He was really proud of it, so we took a picture before we left and he looked really cute as we all trotted into school together.

We arrived at our allotted time of 10 a.m., and he didn't make a fuss at all. He was really happy and excited and went off happily with Mrs Mellor, after a smile and wave back at me.

A few days after Lorcan started, Mrs Mellor called me in to tell me that she had found him really upset while he was playing with his soldiers in the classroom. He hadn't been able to tell her what was wrong but had allowed her to comfort him. When we got home I broached the subject carefully and he managed to tell me that he was upset because he had nobody to play with. That was a horrible feeling and really worried me, but that happens to a lot of children as they move up to school, and he soon had lots of friends.

However, the impact of starting school was worse than we anticipated. Lorcan stopped speaking all over again. For the first few weeks we told ourselves it was OK, that he would improve when he settled in. Then we thought, It's not Christmas yet. Give him a chance. At this point he was talking only to George, and George would speak for him. It wasn't, as you might imagine, that Lorcan whispered in his ear – he wouldn't even have done *that* if someone else was there – but, if anyone came and asked a question, George would pipe up on his behalf. Lorcan has been very lucky, because there is a great group of boys in his class and without them he would have really struggled.

For the teachers, his mutism wasn't a huge problem. He was well behaved and did his work diligently. He would nod or shake his head if asked a question, so they could communicate a little. Bizarrely, he would even put his hand up if he knew the answer to a question but, if the teacher chose him, he wouldn't be able to give the answer. I think he just wanted them to know that he knew it, even though he couldn't say it.

The mutism didn't always stop him from misbehaving either. During the first harvest festival he took part in at school, all the children were singing songs such as 'Big Red Combine Harvester' and behaving like perfect angels, and I watched in horror as Lorcan, who was standing right at the front, directly in front of the new headmistress, shook his fist threateningly at his brother with an evil expression on his face. Then he went one better by sticking his tongue out at members of the audience, people he didn't even know, and pulling silly faces.

In Reception, the staff tried to implement the 'Breaking Down the Barriers' programme, spasmodically. But they hadn't had training and they were just given loads of sheets of paper. I read the sheets and it all sounded so daunting that, if I'm honest, I thought, I'm glad *I* don't have to do it. On the face of it, it looks like really basic games that you play with the kids, getting them to play Guess Who? and other things; but it's much more than that, because you have to push them to a certain limit and then you have to pull back if they don't achieve it. It's very complicated and requires a lot of dedication.

I was having regular meetings with the school because Lorcan has an IEP and, on the advice of the school special-educational-needs coordinator, Mrs Bell, he had been put into 'School Action Plus', a programme for children who need one-to-one help at school. Mrs Bell knew the family well, as she had also taught Adam years before, and it was her job to coordinate interventions, advise the teachers and liaise with the speech-and-language therapist. So instead of parents' evening, where I'd get only a ten-minute slot, I would go for a longer meeting after school. They'd go through the IEP and set Lorcan targets. For example, instead of ignoring the teacher when she called register, they got him to give her the thumbs-up. Another target would be to get him into a group, participating in an activity. His Reception teacher, Mrs Mellor, was wonderful and worked really hard at it, but the school weren't getting the support from the so-called experts.

In December 2009, after the speech therapist discharged Lorcan once again, my husband Dave contacted Dr Anthony John, the recommended paediatrician who deals with autism in our area. Dave told him what the situation was and said, 'Can you see him?' As a professional courtesy, because my husband is a GP, and because we had a history of autism in the family, we got an appointment quickly. Dr John was wonderful and really listened to what we were telling him. But, after we filled in all the forms, he said, 'I don't believe Lorcan has autism, but we can't rule out Asperger's at this stage, as he's too young.' Although there was no diagnosis back then, I was pleased that at least one health professional had acknowledged my fears and observations, and taken me seriously. He also asked the speech therapist to see Lorcan again.

In February, after Dr John's request, the speech-and-language therapist, came to see Lorcan in school and I joined them there. When I arrived at school the class were in the hall doing Circle Time, in which they all sit in a circle and pass an object round, saying something when it comes to them. Both the therapist and I looked suddenly alarmed, wondering what Lorcan would do. Happily, Mrs Mellor knew exactly what she was doing and lots of other children simply passed the toy along and didn't say anything, so Lorcan wasn't alone. When they had finished, Mrs Mellor sent him over to me and, in characteristically theatrical style, Lorcan chose to crawl across the room rather than walk.

The therapist had given me some questions, so Lorcan and I sat down in the school hall, where I went through the assessment with him, while she hid behind a cupboard! The funny thing was that Lorcan knew she was there the whole time, and there was also a teaching assistant with another pupil sitting at a separate table, so it wasn't ideal. He answered all the questions, he scored well, but he whispered every one of his replies to me, and his eyes kept flicking to where the speech therapist was hiding, as if he were thinking, What is that woman doing behind the cupboard? It was a bit bizarre.

He scored well above average on the assessments, so was deemed to have no signs of autism at that time. I disagreed.

Because of Adam, I was convinced that there was more than his just being scared to speak. I could spot some of the signs that I had seen in Adam. For example, Lorcan was very detached from people and disliked cuddles; he was a very neat eater and hated mess on his face; he didn't empathize with people if they hurt themselves; and he found odd things funny, as did Adam. I was totally convinced I had another child on the autistic spectrum.

Because we had such a late diagnosis with Adam's

Asperger's, which had a detrimental effect at school, I didn't want the same thing to happen again. I was determined that, whatever Lorcan's problems were, we should know about them at the earliest possible time, as early intervention is key to helping children deal with autism and to progress.

One day when he was in Reception, I noticed there was a programme about selective mutism on TV, so I recorded it and watched it when Lorcan was in bed. It was really well researched and informative, and quite easy to understand, so I made the decision to show some of the programme to Lorcan.

I had already explained that lots of children have trouble speaking in school and it wasn't just him, but I suspected he didn't really believe me, as he could see all his classmates talking in school and must have wondered why he was the only one who couldn't. To a child of five, that immediate environment is the whole world, so it's hard for them to grab an abstract idea of children they don't know going through the same thing as they are unless they see it for themselves.

One afternoon, we sat down together in the living room and I showed him the programme, which features three girls, all older than he, who also had selective mutism. As he watched it, I watched him for a reaction. One girl, who was ten, was the carbon copy of him – speaking freely and easily at home and totally silent at school. The look on his face when he finally realized there were other children who couldn't speak in school was incredible. It can only be described as pure relief. I was so glad I had decided to let him watch it.

He sat through the rest of the programme with interest, watching intently as they showed how the children, at fifteen, ten and eight, were unable to speak in certain situations and how they made progress throughout the programme. He said very little, just commented on the eight-year-old girl, who couldn't even speak to her grandfather.

'I'm not like that,' he said. 'I can speak to my nana, can't I?'

Towards the end of Reception, Lorcan had begun speaking enough to let Mrs Mellor do some assessments on him. As a result, she gave him a special award for 'making Mrs Mellor proud' and he had to go up in assembly and collect it from the head-teacher, along with some other children who had been given prizes for their own achievements. It's such a lovely way of rewarding individual progress, rather than just rewarding academic grades, and I was really pleased for him.

Typically, though, Lorcan didn't bother telling me he got it. I happened to go rummaging through his bag to look for his reading book and there it was. He had forgotten all about it! I obviously made a huge fuss and praised him, telling him how fantastic it was. He posed for a picture and stuck it up in his room with Blu-Tack. Most children would be desperate to tell their mums they had a head teacher's award, but not Lorcan.

He got the Woodhouse Wonder badge a while later, which is awarded for personal achievement of good behaviour and the child gets to wear for a week. This time he did tell me as soon as he got it. I expect a shiny badge makes more impression on a small boy than a boring certificate.

Lorcan had his fifth birthday at a new play centre, Land of Play, just a few days after he started big school. He chose whom he wanted to invite and, interestingly, he agreed to invite some girls, including Ella. The little group had a whale of a time, charging about madly, climbing and sliding in the soft play area. Lorcan joined in happily and really seemed to be enjoying himself. He sat quietly while they ate the party food and looked pleased as Punch when the *Star Wars* cake was brought in and everybody sang 'Happy Birthday', while he blew out the candles.

A lady from the centre was organizing the party and I had explained about his selective mutism, so she knew what to expect. Lorcan nodded when she asked if he wanted juice but, as expected, he did not speak to her.

After the meal, all the children had a go on some little electric cars but, for the first time that day, Lorcan wouldn't join in. He couldn't explain why he didn't want a go and he even refused to go in one with Luke or his dad. He has never been on one since and has never been able to tell us why.

In February, Mrs Mellor and the teaching assistant Mrs Winterbottom arranged a Valentine's Day tea dance. The parents were asked to come along and what greeted us was a charming sight. Balloons decked the hall, and the tables were laid out nicely, with plates of biscuits, beautifully decorated. As we sat and watched, the Reception children came out in pairs and were introduced by Mrs Mellor. The little boys escorted the girls to their seats, then sat across on the other side of the room from them. The teacher called out each boy's name and asked him to take his partner to the dance floor, and one by one they got up, found the girls they were dancing with and led them out to the centre of the hall. It was all very sweet.

Lorcan looked very reserved at the start but, when his name was called, he duly found his partner, Evie, and got into position – giving me a cheery wave as he waited for the music to start. Then the strains of the Carpenters' 'Top of the World' struck up and they all began to dance around the room. The judges on *Strictly Come Dancing* would have had a field day with some of these little couples. A few just raced around rather than actually dancing and one or two girls were rushed around the floor by their partners at breakneck speed. Lots of spinning children veered towards the party table, where the delicious-looking food was taking their attention away from their fancy footwork.

Lorcan and Evie were very controlled – although they did manage to take a detour around the back of the chairs.

At the end of the first dance, the girls curtsied and the boys bowed. Lorcan stood smiling happily, which was lovely to see. The boys then escorted the girls back to their chairs and Mrs Mellor issued a gentle reminder to the boys that girls didn't necessarily like being dragged around the floor. The next song was 'Never on Sunday' and Lorcan's partner stomped her little heels throughout. During the following track, Lorcan wandered over towards me dragging the poor girl behind him.

Then came the last dance, and the boys collected their partners once more. At this point Evie's little sister decided to join in with the pair, and Lorcan stood frowning crossly while Mrs Mellor went through lots of different songs to find the right one. She chose the Commodores' 'Three Times a Lady' and as soon as they set off again his partner's shoe fell off, which made me laugh. Lorcan came to sit with me for a minute while she sorted herself out and he was clearly having a great time. He smiled and clapped at the end of the dance and then all the children had milk, cakes and biscuits and we were offered a cup of tea and some cake.

The whole afternoon was such a lovely experience for the parents, and it was joy to see the children enjoying the tea dance. We were also given a lovely photograph of Lorcan and Evie, which will always bring back memories of a delightful afternoon, and the thought of Lorcan's beaming face that day still makes me smile.

Lorcan never disliked school. He liked to go, he never cried in the mornings, and he actually seemed to love being there. Mrs Mellor was wonderful with the children, so if there was anything wrong I thought he might be able to go and talk to her, but by the spring he still wasn't speaking properly. He said the odd word and Mrs Mellor heard him speak outside in the school garden, if he thought adults weren't listening. He was making more friends, which was a relief, and George steadfastly stuck by him, helping him every way he could.

It was almost the end of the school year, in the last few weeks of term, before he started to speak again – the same time as the year before.

At the end of the Reception year, I walked past the classroom he was in and the teacher was doing a reading assessment on him – and he was actually saying the words.

It was taking him almost the entire academic year to get comfortable enough – and then we were back to square one every time he went up a year. Even going from Reception to Year One – with exactly the same children in his class and, again, just moving to the classroom next door – set him back again.

Ironically, there are occasions when we wish Lorcan had stayed silent. He has never understood the social niceties when it comes to commenting on people's appearance and, despite his selective mutism, his observations can be incredibly loud when he's talking to me in public.

'Ha ha! Look at that man!' is quite a frequent utterance. He tends to get away with it because he's cute, but it always has me wanting the floor to swallow me whole. When he was two we were in the front garden ripping up weeds and a couple walked past and smiled at Lorcan. As they walked off, he yelled 'Hello, you beggars!' At the top of his voice. Hilarious but totally embarrassing. Fortunately, they were either too polite to react or didn't hear exactly what he said.

At age five, when we were out shopping in Manchester, he shouted, 'Look, there's a dwarf!' Again, we were fortunate that the man in question didn't hear.

On another occasion, we had gone away for a weekend in London, and were staying in a hotel. On our way out one day we waited for a lift on our floor and when it finally arrived, and the doors opened, he commented loudly, 'I can't get in because of all these fat people!' It was very embarrassing, but at least he was taking the weight restriction seriously.

Even at school, he had moments that totally amazed everyone. One playtime, at the age of five, he casually used the F-word in front of the other children. An excited little gaggle of Reception children ran off to tell the teacher – but not because he had used a naughty word. They just couldn't wait to tell her that Lorcan spoke!

At home his constant babble was a frequent source of amusement to us. On one occasion he asked me for a biscuit and then followed up with, 'Lady Mum, Lady Mum, can I have it, please?' And, when I'd told him off about something, he asked Dave, 'Daddy, why is Mummy strict *and* good? Somebody tell me please! Why is Mummy good *and* bad?'

Lorcan is incredibly quick when he's up to something, and on shopping trips you have to watch him like a hawk. He's constantly dodging behind counters in shops and fiddling with the till, or helping himself to 'interesting things'.

At the end of the school year, we were looking forward to a holiday in Disneyland Paris once again, but first we had to get a new passport for

Lorcan. Dave took him to the shopping centre, to a photography shop where they can take your passport photo. Fortunately, the shop was busy, as it was a Saturday.

Lorcan stood very nicely while his photo was taken then they had to wait a few minutes for the pictures and, as usual, he couldn't sit still. He started wandering around 'looking' at things in the shop, including the camera that had been put back on the counter. He is incredibly fast and can swipe things without being noticed. In fact, we always joke he is the Artful Dodger and Luke is Oliver.

After a few minutes of exploring he wandered back to his dad and handed him an object, with a proud, 'Here you go!' Dave looked down and, in his hand, was a piece of equipment from the camera! Lorcan had obviously been fiddling and it had come off. We were just relieved he didn't slip it in his pocket and bring it home. Fortunately, by this time the pictures were ready, so Dave surreptitiously placed the piece of camera on the counter and made a swift exit.

Even at home, there were little treasures that Lorcan would help himself to. When Luke was seven, he was losing lots of milk teeth and Lorcan was fascinated with this and probably a bit jealous – especially after the tooth fairy started doling out cash. One night I crept into Luke's room to swap the tooth for money and carefully delved under his pillow, only to find it was missing. Knowing

Lorcan as well as I do, I went to look under his pillow and, sure enough, there it was. Needless to say, the tooth fairy wasn't impressed and Lorcan went without his ill-gotten gains.

Lorcan is a huge fan of *Deadly 60*, the TV show in which the incredibly brave and rugged animal expert Steve Backshall handles the world's most lethal creatures. He can watch it for hours, fascinated by the dangerous animals.

When we heard Steve's *Live 'n' Deadly* roadshow was going to Liverpool in 2010 we decided to go along, and both boys were really excited. On the day, the rain was pouring down and the boys waited in the downpour patiently for ages, getting soaking wet and very cold. But they got their reward. Eventually, Steve came out and they got to meet him and have a photo with him. Steve spoke to both of them and Luke replied but, of course, Lorcan didn't speak.

Some time later, while playing in the garden, Lorcan noticed some woodlice and, with Luke's help, he wrote a letter to Steve to ask if he would consider including them in his list of *Deadly 60* animals!

Steve kindly sent him an autograph in return, which Lorcan still has, but I'm guessing the woodlice didn't qualify.

Another celebrity encounter came when Lorcan met TV celebrity Matthew Kelly at a demonstration in support of our local hospital, Trafford General, where Lorcan was born. Matthew originates from our district of Urmston and he came back to lend his support to a campaign to save the Accident and Emergency department. He was really lovely and spent ages chatting to locals, and we have some funny pictures of Matthew and Lorcan. One has Lorcan holding a sign with 'Save the birthplace of the NHS' written on it and he's grinning because Matthew is using his head as a leaning post, resting his elbows on it. Again, he never said a word.

At the start of Year One, Lorcan regressed again, despite the class pupils staying the same. This time, it was slightly different because he had a male teacher called Mr Southern, who was brilliant. He made an effort to get to know Lorcan and find out what he was like. He paid him special attention, and that seemed to help a bit.

It was slow progress at first, then, at the first parents' evening, Mr Southern told us he was answering maths questions. He would stick his hand up and actually tell Mr Southern what the answer was, in front of the whole class, but only if it was maths.

One of the traits we noticed in Lorcan, which is also consistent with Asperger's, is that he takes everything absolutely literally, so instructions have to be clear and metaphors or nonliteral phrases simply confuse him.

On one occasion Mr Southern asked, 'Can you take those chairs off the tables?' Lorcan gave him a dirty look and walked off. As far as he was concerned the teacher was asking, 'Are you capable of taking those chairs off the tables?' rather than asking him to do so. Lorcan obviously thought, Yes, of course I can, you fool! From then on, Mr Southern always gave Lorcan clear and proper instructions.

Reading with Lorcan can be quite an experience. A phrase like 'she cried her eyes out' is hilariously funny to him because he imagines exactly that. In one book we were reading, somebody was playing a game of football and the match ended badly, so the text said, 'They blew it.' He didn't understand that this means they didn't win. He pictured them blowing the ball, and he laughs because that's funny. But there may come a point where it won't be funny or he'll be upset because he knows he does not properly understand what is being said.

Lorcan really enjoys the Famous Five books and sometimes finds the language hilariously funny. One night he read, 'Soon there was a fine crackling fire going and the little ruined room was lit by dancing flames.' He thought this very odd, so he started laughing and dancing about.

When Anne – or Annie, as he calls her – comments

on the noise of the sea, saying, 'It really sounds as if it's shouting at the top of its voice', Lorcan immediately said, 'Even though it hasn't got a voice.' So I think he is beginning to understand some similes.

It's amazing how often you use metaphors, similes and slang in everyday conversation, and you don't really notice it until you have a child who takes everything exactly as it sounds. So you might say, 'This bag is so heavy my arm is dropping off.' If Lorcan heard that he might be quite alarmed.

Like any mum, if I'm busy and the kids want anything, I'll say, 'In a minute.' Lorcan takes that as his cue to start counting slowly to sixty, then gets cross if I take a second longer.

Luke was recently telling his brother about something that happened on the school bus that he had found funny. He said, 'I nearly died laughing!'

'Don't be an idiot,' said Lorcan, crossly. 'You didn't nearly die at all.'

Lorcan is also very literal in his own speech, saying exactly what he thinks, even to the point of rudeness. When he was six, a friend of mine, Alison, came to the house and we were chatting on the doorstep. As we talked, I could hear Lorcan shouting 'Mum' over and over, as children do when they don't get any response. 'Mum, I need you,' he insisted. But I could tell there was no emergency, so I carried on chatting. Eventually, he appeared in the hallway, came up to the door and, having never uttered a word to Alison before, demanded, 'Can you please go home?'

In June, with Lorcan making excellent progress at school, we had another appointment with Dr John. This time, we were told he would need a blood test to rule out chromosome abnormalities, so we made an appointment for that.

The nurse came to the house to take a blood sample, and, as we sat there, Lorcan found an ant and played gently with it until she put some 'magic cream' on his arm to numb it for the needle.

As the butterfly needle went towards him I held my breath, expecting a scream any minute. This could send him into one of his meltdowns, I was thinking, apprehensively. To my amazement, he sat, smiling broadly at the nurse, as she stuck the needle in his arm and drew the blood out. There was a clear tube attached, so you could see the blood as it filled up the attached bottle, but he didn't bat an eyelid. The nurses were really thrilled. They're obviously used to children crying and clinging to their mothers, so he must have been the easiest patient they'd ever had!

The blood-test result came back as normal, so that was one thing we didn't need to worry about.

But, strangely, Lorcan's smile often does worry me. He smiles a lot and people don't realize that it's a way of getting through anxious experiences, such as having blood taken, or visiting the dentist. Those who don't know him as we do are often fooled by his beaming face, taking it as a sign he is not anxious when he most definitely is. Selective mutism is a documented anxiety disorder and I don't know whether he uses his smile to disarm people and to appeal to them, or as a coping mechanism to alleviate his anxiety. Either way, it is worrying.

After a year with Mr Southern, Lorcan was once again improving, and we began to think he might make the transition to Year Two without too much of a setback. But in July, just before we broke up for the summer, I was told the school was having a reshuffle and the teacher who had taught Year Two for years was moving to Year Five. I was absolutely devastated. Mrs Stevens was one of the reasons I chose that particular school for the boys. She is an amazing teacher and I hoped she could work her magic on Lorcan.

The news left me really down and upset about the whole thing and suddenly my fears that Lorcan would never be able to speak in school like other children, and the worry that he would fall behind with his work, began to overwhelm me. Of course, I had to act. I wrote a strongly worded letter to the new head teacher expressing my anger and upset. As soon as she received it, she phoned me and we had a long and very promising conversation, which ended with Lorcan being allocated three sessions a week with the Year Two teacher to focus on the 'Breaking Down the Barriers' programme.

Although I am a practical person, and like to deal with problems head on, there have been times when I have been emotional about Lorcan's selective mutism. It can be distressing when you take your child somewhere and he can't speak because, as I mentioned, it is an anxiety disorder. As a parent, I find it upsetting to know that he's feeling anxious or distressed, but I tend to just deal with things in a pragmatic way. At the end of the day, it's not about me: it's about Lorcan.

CHAPTER 5

SMITTEN WITH THE KITTEN

In September, 2010, our poor old moggy, Flo, became seriously ill with kidney failure. She began crying to me and coming to me more than usual and was weeing a lot more often. On one occasion, I cleaned her litter tray and forgot to bring it back into the house. The clever cat peed in a plastic bowl I'd left on the floor, which turned out to be very useful as the vet needed a sample and it saved her having to go through the trauma of our trying to get one. Not an easy task, as you can imagine.

The vet said her kidneys were failing, so they suggested it would be kindest to put her to sleep. She was fourteen and had been going downhill for a while, so we had known this day was going to come, but Dave and I were really upset when she went because she'd been part of the family for such a long time. I couldn't stay in the room while she was put down, but Adam and my mum stayed. Adam, who had had Flo since he was a child, was obviously badly affected, as she was really his cat. When she was cremated, he wanted the ashes, so they put them in a beautiful container with ribbon around it and he put them in his bedroom.

Some time later, on one of Lorcan's rummaging sessions in Adam's room, he came across the ashes and was intrigued. He tried to open the container to see 'Flo's bones and blood' and from then on we had to hide them!

Because the antics of the younger two had always sent her scurrying upstairs for peace and quiet, they had never really had a proper relationship with Flo, as they had with the dog. We knew they wouldn't be too devastated, so we took the opportunity to explain about death, very casually, and they were quite interested. Lorcan wasn't that bothered at all, just wanted to take a look at her.

As soon as she was gone, I wanted another cat, but it had to be the right one. Before Flo we'd had cats who were run over and, with Flo, I kept her in for a very long time at the beginning of her life because she was a winter kitten. By the time she had been spayed she wasn't really bothered about the great outdoors. She went outside but she never went beyond the garden, which was great, and probably why she lasted until she was fourteen.

We decided to get a replacement straightaway. Much as I love the dog, I've always been more of a cat person, so there was never any doubt that I would get another one. I thought, Right. I don't want a cat that goes out and roams about. If I get a pedigree I won't even be tempted to let it out.

If you're not careful with kittens, someone ends up leaving the door open and they escape and I didn't want any harm coming to her.

Not being one to hang around, I started looking on the day Flo was put to sleep. I wasn't sure what breed to get, so, as I did with Lily, I kept looking at different cats on the websites, and I filled in the online questionnaires that help you decide which cat you want. They ask whether you're prepared to groom it, if it needs to be good with kids and these sorts of things, and they come up with breeds.

The two that kept cropping up were Birman and Maine Coon – but the latter apparently needs a lot of grooming, so I wasn't very keen on that. So that really left a Birman. I read up a bit more to see if they had any hereditary problems, because some pedigree cats have heart troubles and other medical issues. Birmans got a clean bill of health.

The next step was to find a breeder. I tracked down two who were reasonably close to home and contacted them on the first day of my search. One of them, a lady called Janet Bowen, got back to me straightaway and said her cat had recently had a litter and she had one female left. I didn't stop to ask how old she was, or what colour she was, even though they are all different shades, and Janet didn't say much at all, but she was only in Chorley, Lancashire, which is a short pop up the motorway, so I said, 'Oh wonderful. Can I come and see it?'

The following night, when David got in from work, my mum came round to look after the kids while we went off to look at the cat. We decided not to take the children because we didn't think we were going to get a cat immediately, and we didn't want them disappointed if we decided against the kitten for any reason. The intention was just to have a look, but we stuck the cat box in the car just in case.

When we arrived, the breeder opened the door and she had this kitten on her shoulder, a tiny little blob of fluff. We walked into the house and a beautiful adult Birman, who turned out to be the kitten's mum, greeted us. Janet also had a black moggy who was really lovely – and then all these kittens charging around and jumping off the furniture. It was years since I'd seen Flo jump or climb on anything and I found it fascinating to watch them all playing.

Feeling a little overprotective, I was saying, 'Ooh, are they allowed to jump off those?' She laughed at me and said, 'Yes, of course.'

As we sat there watching, I suddenly thought, I really want two – but that's really silly and extravagant. Although she was an average price for her breed, this kitten was by no means cheap at £400. As if she read my mind, Janet offered us a discount if we took two.

'Do you want me to go to the bank?' said David, obviously smitten himself.

'No!' I said, emphatically. 'Don't be daft.'

I don't know what discount he was expecting but I'm guessing it wouldn't have been huge. And then there would be double vets' bills, food bills and so on. Pets are not cheap to look after, so I persuaded myself that one would have to be enough. As Jess was the only female, we chose her. She was such an amazingly cute little bundle, with creamy white fur, a little dark face and the prettiest blue eyes. She was irresistible. We couldn't leave her behind, so we loaded her into our cat box and brought her straight home.

When we got home the children were still up and itching to meet the new member of the family. The first thing I did was make sure the dog was shut away, for obvious reasons. Lily had been frightened of Flo, because she used to put her paw out at her as a warning. It hadn't been in a very aggressive way, but it had been enough to tell Lily who was boss. But Flo had been an adult cat when Lily was a puppy, and she made it clear that she was the one encroaching on *her* territory, and she wasn't going to put up with any nonsense. It was different with Jess, because she was so tiny when we got her and she was coming into Lily's space so we weren't sure how Lily would react.

When Lily was out of the way, I put the cat box on the floor and opened it, and this tiny little fluffy kitten popped out. She was such an appealing little thing, and they'd never seen a really young kitten close up before, so everyone was just besotted. She was absolutely gorgeous and super-friendly. We had friends who came round to see the new kitten and, instead of scratching or bolting when strangers picked her up, she just sat there and allowed herself to be stroked, or she would pop up on the sofa and curl up on the kids' knees. They were fascinated by her.

Lorcan fell under Jessi's spell the moment we brought her home. The delight on his face when he saw her pop out of the cat carrier was lovely to see. She was tiny and very pretty and, best of all for Lorcan, she happily submitted to being picked up and carried.

Most kittens object to small children handling them, and kids can be quite rough, but the Birman breed are known to be good with children. Jessi has always been a placid, tolerant cat. Kittens are very sociable little beings and are attracted by movement and the high pitch of a child's voice. As Lorcan has always been a busy little person, Jess found plenty of interest in the things he got up to. She wanted to get involved with all his activities. Whether he was charging round the house playing Indiana Jones or playing with toys in the playroom, Jess was there.

The close bond between Lorcan and Jessi-cat developed very quickly and surprised us all. I never expected in a million years that he would react in such a positive way. We got the dog when Lorcan was around three, and he really loves her, but the gentleness he shows Jessi is rarely shown to Lily. He is really rough with her, wrestling her, getting her in a headlock and playing roughly, but Lily doesn't seem to mind.

With Jess, from the very start, he was as gentle as can be. He seemed to know that you can't play rough with a kitten, as he does with Lily. He treated her very tenderly and soon began speaking to her in a special voice, as if she were a tiny child. He quickly became very protective of Jess, and still gets very cross with people if he thinks they are 'being mean' to her.

'Are you OK, Jess?' he asks sweetly. 'Were they being mean to you?'

When I was a child my first kitten had been rescued by my mum when it was being chased by a dog, and she had decided to keep it. My brother and I were asked to pick a name but we couldn't agree, so the poor thing never had a name. It was called Ch or Cat for its entire life. When we knew we were getting a kitten I couldn't bear the thought of the three of them arguing over cat names, as my brother and I had, so I decided I would choose the name and present it as a fait accompli.

Lorcan had a much-treasured cuddly toy, which was Jess, the cat from *Postman Pat*. It was bought for me by Adam originally but Lorcan became attached to it, so he had kind of adopted it. I thought about that toy and I liked the name, so

I told them the cat was called Jess as soon as we brought her home. Lorcan was really pleased, since she had the same name as his cuddly toy. Even so, over the next few weeks, Jess became Jessi, Jessica and then Jessi-cat.

As I mentioned, her pedigree name is Bluegenes Angel.

Jess was twelve weeks old when she came to us and was already litter-trained, so she was no bother at all. They're not like a puppy, which needs a walk and a little bit more attention. With cats you just feed them, clear their litter and they're happy. But Jess got plenty of attention from Lorcan, and she soon returned the affection. They quickly became inseparable. She followed him around the house, came looking for him when she heard him laugh, and greeted him at the door when he came home from school.

Lorcan has always been fascinated by the World Wars and armies. He has lots of small toy soldiers and even went to the school party to mark the wedding, in April 2011, of Prince William and Kate Middleton – now the Duke and Duchess of Cambridge – dressed in a soldier outfit. In fact, one year, my homemade Mother's Day card featured a soldier with a gun!

When Jess was a kitten, Lorcan loved to play on the floor with his fort and his little soldier figures. He would clear a big space in the playroom, which is where Lorcan spends a lot of his time, and spend ages carefully setting them up in neat rows, as if they were in battle. Jess would carefully walk through dozens of little figures set up in battle formation, or occasionally she would show her mischievous side and charge through, knocking them over!

Funnily enough, Lorcan never told her off for spoiling his game. If the dog or one of the family had done the same, he would have been furious and we would probably have been told we were a 'pea brain' or 'jerk', or another of his favourite insults. But with Jess he would laugh or give her a gentle scolding.

I once filmed the pair of them playing soldiers in the playroom. Lorcan was methodically setting up the ranks when she jumped across and devastated the whole scene, leaving soldiers lying everywhere, like the aftermath of a fierce battle. Lorcan patiently began to pick them up, one by one, and he had barely managed to get two or three upright when she charged through again. This time he whipped them away, just in time, then started putting them all back, all over again. If it had been Luke or I who had knocked them over he would have been furious, but he just said, 'Stop it, Jess,' and carried on.

Another favourite game the terrible twosome soon discovered involved an Indiana Jones whip that Lorcan had as part of a dressing-up costume. He charges through the house with that as she chases behind, and that will keep them both occupied for hours.

As well as struggling to express emotions, Lorcan suffers from extremes in his moods. He's either really happy and singing or full of doom and gloom and devastated, crying and having a tantrum. There's no middle ground, a fact that was picked up on by the educational psychologist when we eventually saw her, later. As a result, Lorcan can be loud – really loud – especially if he's crying or throwing a real strop. He will scream at the top of his voice. But his laughter is loud, too. I can be in a deep sleep in my bedroom and Lorcan will wake me up because I can hear his laugh, all the way from the living room downstairs. He also has a very high-pitched voice, and I think some cats would shrink away from him when he's being too noisy, because they don't like loud noises, but Jess doesn't seem to be bothered. The dog will move away if he's crying and screaming, but Jess stays beside him. She won't go and try to comfort him, but she won't move away from him, either, and just her being there seems to be a soothing presence.

If cats have nine lives, then Jess has only six left. She used up the other three before she'd reached her first birthday.

For the first few months she was at home, I took

Jess up to bed at night because I wasn't entirely comfortable leaving her around the dog. Lily was a bit jealous and I thought she might swipe her with a paw or even bite the back of her neck, because dogs can do that to try to show their dominance. She was such a tiny little thing that I was determined to keep an eye on her.

On the night we brought her home, the dog had been very interested in her and didn't seem likely to hurt her, but I wasn't taking any chances just yet. So I popped Jess in her bed and took her upstairs with us. As I set her down on the floor, she hopped up on the bed and settled down for the night on my pillow, and I didn't have the heart to shoo her off, so I eased gingerly into bed beside her and left her there.

In the morning, I couldn't see her at first and then I found her squished between my pillows, not moving. A feeling of absolute horror washed over me. I really thought she had suffocated, and I went completely cold. Then I shrieked, 'I've killed her! I've killed her!' Dave calmly picked her up and she opened her eyes blinking and yawning. Phew!

A few days later, curiosity nearly killed the cat when she fell in the bath. I didn't even think that cats liked water, so I didn't think about shutting the door as I filled the tub for a nice long soak. I came into the bathroom to find a very surprised, bedraggled kitten jumping onto the bathmat, absolutely dripping wet. She was such a sorry sight. She'd fallen in and somehow managed to save herself by scrambling back up the side, but I like a very deep bath, so she could easily have drowned.

Jess was such a beautiful and loving cat that lots of people we knew wanted us to let her have kittens, so they could have one, but we decided against it because it can be dangerous for the cat, and I'm such a softy I would probably insist on keeping them all anyway. So, when she was six months old, I took her in to get spayed, as I have with all our animals. It's a routine op, and I didn't anticipate any problems so I left her and went home, having arranged to pick her up later.

That afternoon we received a phone call from the vet, who said, 'She's OK now but her heart stopped when they put her under anaesthetic.' I was thinking, What am I going to tell the kids if she dies? What am I going to do?

I was panic-stricken. They wanted permission to take X-rays to check for cardiac anomalies and said they were keeping her in overnight for observation. We were all so attached to Jessi by now that the thought of losing her was devastating.

Fortunately, the X-rays were fine and they decided the anaesthetic drugs they used were not suitable for her. Plus, the vet thought she was a Ragdoll – a different breed of cat, which is known to have heart problems – and I think she panicked. Jess wasn't spayed on that occasion and we spent many months after this deciding whether to have her neutered or not. Eventually, I saw a different vet and said, 'What would you do?' and he said, 'I'd use a different drug.' We went ahead with it and, this time, she was fine, but I was pretty shaken because I would never have thought that she would be in danger of dying on the operating table when she was just getting spayed. That was quite traumatic.

Thankfully she has managed to survive all these near-death experiences and, at that time, nobody knew what an impact this lovely cat would have on our lives.

CHAPTER 6

UNBREAKABLE BOND

Jessi-cat has always been a house cat. We do let her in the garden but only under constant supervision, and Lorcan loves to watch her play there, so he's always outside when she wants to go out.

On the first few trips outside she spent her time exploring, climbing up trees and being rescued and wandering around, in and out of the flower-beds. Then one afternoon, as Lorcan played with her outside, she suddenly hopped onto the fence and disappeared. She was gone in a flash and we were frantic. We called her but she didn't come and we couldn't find her anywhere, so we spent the next two hours knocking on our neighbours' doors and shouting her name up and down the street. Eventually, she was spotted a few doors away, having a wonderful time chasing butterflies among the flowerbeds, oblivious to the fuss she'd caused.

In April 2011, six months after she arrived, it was a lovely spring day, so we took Jess out into the garden and she spent a few happy moments eating grass and sniffing around, as she likes to do. Usually, she is content to stay where she's supposed to be, but on this particular day her mischievous side took over, and she decided to cause another commotion.

Luke and Lorcan were supervising her in the garden while I was busy cleaning the litter tray – I do lead a glamorous life! Suddenly I heard the boys shrieking and yelling and when I went outside Lorcan was just coming into the house, looking worried.

'Jess is up a tree! She can't get down,' he told me, excitedly.

I went out to investigate and saw Jess clinging to a branch about twelve feet up the tree in our back garden. Luke, who is a keen climber of trees, clambered up as far as he could but still couldn't reach her. We were getting worried, because she was miaowing miserably, clinging on and looking very unstable, as if she could fall any minute.

'Go inside and get Adam,' I said. With Dave at work Adam was the tallest in the house, so I was hoping he could help avoid our making that clichéd call to the fire brigade. With a great deal of effort, Adam managed to climb up and rescue the stranded kitten, who seemed grateful to be on solid ground again. We kept her inside for a while after that.

A fortnight later, I came downstairs in the morning to find Jessi-cat zooming round the house looking really excited. She was obviously chasing something and, when I looked closer, I could see it was a fly. She spent about two hours stalking it and leaping at it. By the time she caught it we were all watching her in fascination. As she is an indoor cat, we weren't used to seeing her acting like a 'real' cat, hunting and stalking her prey.

Eventually, the fly was cornered, buzzing around the window in the living room. Hunter Jess pounced and caught it. We were all so pleased for her that we broke into a spontaneous round of applause. Of course, I then had to remove her half-dead victim.

When Lorcan was tiny he loved the Mog books by Judith Kerr. Mog, as you would expect, is a cat, and is the main character in the series – so he has always liked cats – but we soon realized the bond between these two was something very special. Jessi-cat started spending a lot of time in Loran's bedroom and she loved to sleep on a furry quilt we bought for him a little while back. If I was reading to Lorcan at night, Jess would come and curl up on the bed, as if she wanted to listen with him.

At night, Lorcan still arranged the cuddly-toy guard round his bed but now, during the day, I would often find a crowd of monkeys on the bed surrounding him and Jessi. The monkeys were on guard and Jess would be the princess. Or Jess might spend half an hour sitting on her cat tree knocking fluffy mice off for Lorcan to pick up, which he did patiently and endlessly, as you would for a toddler.

In the playroom is a cardboard castle for Jess, which she climbs inside while she's playing with Lorcan. She peeps out of the windows and he likes to dangle her toys for her to catch. Lorcan laughs hysterically when she swipes at the toys with her paw as he yells, 'Look at Jessi – she's slaying the baddies!'

But Jess was becoming much more than a plaything to Lorcan. He soon began to involve her in everything he was doing and, more importantly, to talk to her, constantly.

Whenever Jess came into the room, he'd start to chatter away. He would tell her about his day, what he'd learned at school and so on.

Although he talked to Jess, he never really revealed too much about his feelings, because I don't think he can, to anyone. If I say, 'How was school?' he'll say, 'Rubbish.' But if I ask, 'Why was it rubbish?' he'll just say anything to shut me up. You can never really tell what's going on inside.

Lorcan can't say whether or not he's had a bad day at school, as other children would. If his teacher is on a course and they have a supply teacher, he'll be OK, but he's more whingey when he comes home, and that's how we know something is up. He can't tell me straight. He wouldn't be able to say, 'I didn't like that new lady.' And that's one of the things that worry me, because, equally, he wouldn't tell me if he was being bullied or someone did something to upset him.

Even with Jess, he didn't tell her any profound

things such as, 'Today this happened and I didn't like it.' But he seemed to love the fact that he got a vocal response from her every time he told her anything. She has a very loud miaow, and would respond to his chatter with it, which made him chat even more.

When he was down on the floor with his action figures, he gave her a running commentary on the battle he was enacting. He would tell her, 'This soldier in green is fighting this one in black,' and show her who were the good guys and who were the bad ones. And he would constantly ask questions, seeming quite happy that the miaow he got in return was the answer he was looking for.

Like a little magpie, Lorcan has always been attracted to shiny 'treasures'. When he was seven we were at my mum's house and he went upstairs to the toilet, then came down loaded up with jewellery. He had numerous bracelets up his arms and a ring on every finger. When it was time to go home, they had to be prised off him under considerable protest. He tried to negotiate keeping 'just this tiny thing', which happened to be a heavy, twenty-two-carat wedding ring but, needless to say, we refused. As soon as he got home, he couldn't wait to complain to Jessi-cat.

'Meany Nana wouldn't let me keep that little gold thing,' he told her. He got the required sympathetic miaow and he made a beeline for the ring every time we visited my mum after that.

When Lorcan came home from school, Jess would come down to find him. She doesn't sleep a huge amount, as some cats do, but wanders around the house looking for amusement. She would seek him out in his bedroom and we could hear, as soon as she was there, because he starts chatting away in a little singsong voice, telling her everything. Hearing that sound always puts a smile on my face because I know that his chat to Jess can only be a positive thing.

We have a photograph of Lorcan that I happened to capture as he came home from after-school football. He is in football kit and kneeling on the floor, to take off his muddy boots. Jess just walked up to him and touched him with her nose on his nose. It's the sweetest image and all the more heart-rending because, while he doesn't like being touched by me or Dave, he doesn't mind being touched by the animals, and especially Jess.

Jess does all the usual cat things such as sitting on the laptop keyboard, scurrying through people's legs when they are going upstairs, scratching wallpaper and hiding from the vacuum cleaner. We also have to check the washing machine and tumble dryer before we use them, every time, because she often crawls in there for a sleep.

She hates the sound of the hoover, so she runs away and hides when I'm using it, then reappears when it is switched off. If I'm mopping the floor she chases the mop around, which makes the job take twice as long.

Lorcan was watching me mopping the kitchen floor recently and asked if he could have a go. I showed him how to do it and told him how to clean it without standing on it and dirtying it again. I left him to it. Jess was having tons of fun chasing the mop around, and Lorcan started shouting to me, 'Jessi keeps walking on the clean floor with her filthy feet! Whatever are we to do?' He was smiling when he said it and secretly loved having Jessi 'help' with the mopping.

On one occasion, I decided to rearrange the bookshelf but Jess thought she'd get in on the action, so she crawled in there and sat on the books. In the end I had to give up!

Our phone is in the hall and if I am on it she makes a real nuisance of herself. She jumps up onto the cupboard and starts miaowing really loudly, rubbing her head against the phone. She has cut me off a few times by stepping on the phone. It is also awkward if I'm trying to write down instructions or jot down notes while on the phone as she nudges the pen out of my hand. I can't even lock her in the living room because she can open all the doors.

She loves anything fluffy or feathery, so we have to be careful what we leave lying around. I have a favourite scarf that has little pompoms on it and, for several weeks, I kept finding it at the top of the stairs, and then at the bottom of the stairs, and it didn't take a Sherlock Holmes to work out who had been playing with it. I always left it at the end of the bed but it could end up anywhere in the house by the time she'd finished with it.

Ever the mischievous moggy, she torments the poor dog by winding her up and getting Lily to chase her. Despite my misgiving at the beginning of their relationship, Jess stands her ground now and they fight and chase, but it's all very playful. Even though Jess is always the instigator, Lily is the one who gets into trouble with Lorcan. He doesn't like it and he always tells Lily off, with a firm, 'Stop it, Lily. You're hurting Jess!'

When Jess wants something she'll let you know in no uncertain terms by making herself heard. She'll miaow incredibly loudly when she wants to be picked up and she likes to be messed with and fussed over. She's a demon for a bit of petting. Lorcan doesn't pick her up too much, because I don't like the way he picks her up. She ends up hanging with her front legs squashed into her body. She doesn't mind – although a lot of cats would have a go, or complain – but I can't bear to watch it, so I just say, 'Put her down. She doesn't look too happy about being held like that.' But he can mess about with her and she follows him everywhere, so he doesn't need to pick her up that much. If he's sitting down watching TV she'll come and sit with him or lie next to him on the sofa.

Jess is a curious cat and likes to know what you're doing. If I'm in the house on my own and pottering around, getting on with housework, she will come and find me, wherever I am. She likes company, she likes people, so she seeks them out. But grown-ups are really boring, because they're cooking, or sitting down talking, and doing nothing of interest. Because the boys have got lots of toys and fun things, she prefers being around them and she seeks out things that she finds interesting in their rooms. She jumps up onto the cupboards and shelves, to have a sniff around, and knocks every-thing off in the process.

Jess seems pretty intelligent. She soon learned her name and, when she slept in our room, I would say, 'Bed, Jess,' and she would obediently trot off upstairs.

Although we had her upstairs at night for a while, she sleeps anywhere she likes now. Our bedroom door doesn't shut properly but I push it closed and then I hear a little creak and then silence, and in she walks. I can be sitting reading and, every time she sees me there, she looks startled. She knows I've come upstairs, so I have no idea why she's so surprised.

Even people who visit who don't like cats take to Jess. I've got a friend who really doesn't like them – except for Jess. She wouldn't cuddle her but she's fascinated by her. I think it's those piercing blue eyes, that are so unusual.

In April 2011, Lorcan started Beaver Scouts – the youngest section of the scouting movement in Britain – with two friends from school. Luke had already been going for a while, and had moved up to cubs, so Lorcan went quite happily, since he had often been there when we dropped his brother off. The leaders were all familiar to Lorcan and I had explained the selective mutism to them, so they were very understanding.

They knew Lorcan couldn't say the Beaver Promise out loud, so they allowed him to write it down himself and got someone else to read it out for him. He really enjoyed the weekly meetings but, when they started to go on full-day trips, he didn't feel he was able to go. He did manage a short trip with them on a woodland walk, which was real progress, so we were really pleased.

The summer after he joined, Beaver Scouts invited Lorcan's troop to one of the bigger camps, Bispham Hall near Wigan, for a day-long district event called a Celebration of Scouting Excellence. Lorcan agreed to go only because parents were invited, so we went along too. The boys were encouraged to try different activities such as shooting, which Lorcan enjoyed and participated in, but he drew the line at sledging down a muddy hill, and refused to take part.

Afterwards the children got a certificate of attendance and Lorcan was thrilled by that.

In August 2011, just before Lorcan embarked

on another daunting class change, we had another appointment with the community paediatrician, Dr John. We told him that the speech-and-language therapist had taken us off the books, again, and he was quite annoyed. He rang the therapist and asked, 'What is the point of developing a programme for the school, if nobody follows it up?' He also wrote a letter outlining Lorcan's case. He wrote, 'At Beaver Scouts a friend speaks for Lorcan, as in the biblical relationship between Moses and his brother Aaron.' Not being a very religious person, I had to look up the story because I had never heard it. Apparently Aaron was the one to address the people on behalf of Moses, because he could 'speak well'. It struck me it could also describe the relationship between Luke and Lorcan.

I was glad he acknowledged that Lorcan went to Beavers. I often felt when I visited doctors and experts, that they suspected I wasn't allowing him to do the things other boys do, but he's been going to Beavers since he was six and is now in Cubs. He also loves football and spends a great deal of his time kicking a ball, just like any other boy.

When Lorcan was three Dave had a season ticket for Manchester City and he took the two boys to a football match. It was a pre-season game between City and Valencia, at the City of Manchester Stadium, which has now been renamed the Etihad Stadium.

As they were settling in their seats near the pitch side, there were cheers from the crowds behind them. Looking back, they saw that the crowd reaction was for the arrival of Ricky Hatton, the former welterweight champion, who lives in Manchester. Dave offhandedly mentioned to Luke and Lorcan who he was, then he and Luke settled to enjoy the football. Lorcan proceeded to spend the entire first half with his back to the pitch trying to see this 'famous person' and totally ignored the football.

Lorcan has always had an interest in football but he's pretty fickle when it comes to supporting a team. He has shown an interest in Chelsea and Stoke previously but that's only because he liked the sound of their names! He has a football-sticker album and he can name all the players. He also has both a Manchester City shirt and a Manchester United shirt, which is a bit of a no-no in Manchester. He's very much a floating supporter.

In Year Two, he joined the after-school football club on Thursday evenings and last summer holidays he insisted on going to a football summer school at his primary school. He was familiar with the coach who teaches sport in school and some of his friends were going. I was really surprised, as it was all day for two weeks, but it was really great for him, as he was socializing with unfamiliar people and getting exercise, but mainly having plenty of fun. He had to take a packed lunch and go in football kit and, Lorcan being Lorcan, he went wearing a wild variety of mix-and-match strips. Once he went wearing one Ireland football sock, an England sock, City shorts and a United shirt!

It was after one of these days that I got the picture of Jessi giving him a proper kitty greeting by touching her nose on his.

He enjoyed the soccer school but when he started back at school in September I asked if he wanted to do after-school football.

'No, it's boring,' he said.

'But I thought you loved it,' I said, surprised.

'I just want to play matches, not do the other boring stuff.' Basically, he meant he enjoyed the games but he didn't want to do the warm-up exercises, skills training and fitness training. Later, I spoke to a speech therapist about this and she suggested that it was probably an Asperger's thing, not understanding the need to learn the skills in order to play better, but wanting to play the match. However I have spoken to other parents who have said their children were the same at that age and went back to football later with added enthusiasm. He still enjoys playing football at home and will happily boot a ball around the house until I chase him outside.

Last year, we managed to have a nosy in one of the boxes at Old Trafford – home of Manchester United – because we were at an event there. Lorcan enjoyed looking at the pitch and poking about in cupboards but left his own little souvenir for them: dozens of small grubby hand prints all over the viewing window, which had been immaculate when we arrived.

Dr John in his letter added that we could not treat the communication difficulty unless its cause was understood. He concluded, 'The expected outcome is positive, providing Lorcan's anxieties are the focus of the attention, i.e. not speech-focused.'

As a result, Lorcan was finally seen by a new speech-and-language therapist, who had some experience of selective mutism, and she gave excellent support to his school.

Dr John was still concerned about Lorcan's continuing struggle at school and he believed Lorcan should be 'statemented' – issued with a statement of Special Educational Needs (SEN), which, in turn, could mean support and funding for the school to help him get the best out of his education. This, I agreed, would become even more crucial when he progressed from primary to secondary school – a move that terrified me, in the light of the trauma I knew Adam had been through in his teenage years.

As soon as I got home from the appointment, I wrote to Trafford Local Education Authority requesting the SEN statement. A few weeks later, I received an extremely unhelpful letter which began, 'Dear Mrs Dillan'. So they had spelled my name wrong, a shabby start, to say the least. It went on to say, 'According to the Special Education Needs code of practice, medical diagnosis of disability does not necessarily imply that a child has special education needs.' In other words, bog off!

Fancy sending that letter out to a worried parent. I wasn't happy. Naturally, that wasn't the last they were to hear from me.

CHAPTER 7

THREE LITTLE WORDS

One afternoon, about six months after we got Jess, I was sitting reading a paper in our living room and Lorcan and Jess were playing happily on the floor with her favourite green feather toy. Suddenly, I heard Lorcan utter an astonishing phrase. 'I love you, Jessi-cat.' Then he added, 'You are my best friend.' I couldn't believe my ears and a tear sprang to my eyes. It was the first time I'd ever heard him say those three little words, and I really didn't mind that they weren't directed at me.

As I said, Lorcan has never been able to express his emotions. He would never say, 'I love you' to me, and that's fine. He expresses his love in funny ways, such as downloading a game for me on my iPad or bringing me a biscuit when I'm having a cup of tea, but I know he loves me, so I don't need to hear him say it out loud. Even so, to hear him tell Jess was a surprise, but it was so sweet, a really cute moment. I even had a few butterflies in my tummy as various emotions flitted through me. Overwhelmingly, I was happy for him, because you can't just keep all your emotions inside you. It can't be good to keep everything locked up inside, and I'm sure it could lead to trouble later on. You have to learn to express emotions, whether that means you scream and have an angry strop or express things more calmly.

Part of my surprise stemmed from the fact that Lorcan always misses out 'soppy' words when he is reading, or changes them to something less embarrassing. He also does this with girls' names, which he finds silly, and he covers his eyes if he sees anyone on TV kissing – even animated Disney characters. So to hear him tell Jessi he loves her was something of a breakthrough. It was and still is of huge importance to us. It can be used as a building block to teach Lorcan about emotions, which is important for his mental wellbeing.

People have often asked me if I was upset that Lorcan can tell the cat that he loves her but can't tell me. I can honestly say that I really don't feel that way. I just think it's healthy for him that he can express his love for Jess, because he can't do that with people. My hope is that he might learn to do that with people eventually, or at least learn that's how you get on better in life, by expressing certain feelings or reactions, even if it's not genuine. He doesn't react the way that society dictates you should, because he doesn't tend to see other people's perspectives. With Jess, he can. If the dog is chasing her and she's squealing a bit – even if they're playing – Lily gets told off by Lorcan, because he knows Jess is smaller and more delicate, and has to be looked after. So the affinity he has with her has taught him to see situations from a point of view other than his own.

Another trait he has, which is common in those on the autistic spectrum, is the inability to sympathize with other people's pain or upset. I once fell down the stairs and, although I didn't do myself any real damage, I really hurt my ankle and I was crumpled at the bottom of the stairs crying with pain.

Both Luke and Lorcan were about two yards away from me in the living room and Luke came rushing out to see what was wrong. Lorcan stayed exactly where he was, playing a game on his iPad. He was oblivious of the whole thing. That is a result of the Asperger's, and Adam would have been the same at Lorcan's age. Now he's older, Adam has taught himself the right way to react if someone is in trouble, or is hurt. He was out recently with a friend in Edinburgh and the friend had an epileptic fit, so Adam had to deal with it, look after him and ring the ambulance, but he knew that was the correct response and he coped well.

People often think those on the autistic scale don't feel any empathy at all. I thought the same, especially while I lay in a heap at the bottom of the stairs. I was really distressed and a bit shocked that he didn't react at all. But it's not that they don't feel empathy: it's just that they can't express it and don't know how to react to it, which all fits in where Lorcan is concerned.

If he kicked me by accident, he would just laugh it off. He wouldn't say sorry or worry that he'd hurt me, whereas Luke would automatically say, 'I'm really sorry, Mum. Are you OK?' But it's a different story when he's around Jess. If Lorcan bumps into her he'll say, 'Sorry, Jess. I'm really sorry,' and then he will stroke her and make a fuss. Lorcan only behaves like that with the cat. He may have learned these things from Luke, and from others, but he still doesn't do it around people.

Mind you, he must have learned something from the stair incident – if only how to scare the living daylights out of me. One afternoon, I was in the bathroom upstairs when I heard huge bangs and crashes, so I rushed out to see what disaster had befallen him. Lorcan was splayed out at the bottom of the stairs, so I ran down in a panic to check if he was OK, at which point the little menace started laughing. He'd arranged himself at the bottom of the stairs to trick me!

From the first time he told Jess he loved her it became a regular occurrence.

He will be playing on the floor with her and, quite spontaneously, he'll say, 'I love you, Jess.' He'll ask her how she is, and chat to her about what he's doing in a really sweet way. He cuddles her and even kisses her – and he would never kiss me in a million years.

In the months after his first declaration of love, I watched him interact with our gorgeous cat and I began to realize how special this relationship was for him. Seeing this little boy enjoying such a close bond with his pet was heartwarming and brought a tear to the eye. Lorcan obviously feels comfortable with Jess – in a way he doesn't always feel around people – and he is devoted to her. She is highly responsive, miaowing appropriately and rubbing her head on Lorcan and his toys. She greets him at the door when he comes in from school and sometimes by rubbing her nose on his.

If Lorcan is upset he goes to find Jess to seek comfort. He will look sad and say, 'I want Jessi.' Then he will seek her out and cuddle her. He also does this if he thinks he is in trouble. Lorcan is very responsive to smiles and gets confused if someone is cross with him. If we use a stern voice he thinks we are shouting at him, even when we are not.

I often wonder whether the more obvious vocal responses Jess gives Lorcan are more noticeable to him and, therefore, touch him more than the more subtle reactions he gets from the dog. Maybe that is why he responds differently to the two pets.

The summer after Jess arrived, Adam had to have an operation and, when he came out of hospital, Dave took the two younger boys to Ireland for a long weekend, to give Adam some peace and quiet while he recovered.

He had previously taken Luke on his own but never both. This time, though, there was no screaming on the ferry and both were well behaved. Lorcan can be a menace but Luke is a great help in looking after him, and Lorcan was becoming more familiar with the Irish side of the family, who are wonderful with him. He didn't speak directly to people but he chatted away happily in front of them, and he had a lovely time.

One day Dave and the kids went to visit his sister, Marie Louise, who had a young baby. At one point, Dave noticed that Lorcan had disappeared. He went in search to find him making himself at home in the baby's bedroom, having a good look at things and examining baby toys.

It was the first time Lorcan had been away without me, so, when they all got back, I was anxious to see him. Luke gave me a hug but Lorcan made a beeline for the animals and said, 'Hello, Jessi. Hello, Lily!' He picked Jessi up and gave her cuddle – and then, finally, he noticed me and gave me a big grin.

The rest of that summer holiday we decided to fill the time with family day trips. On one beautiful day in August, we took the boys to Blackpool zoo.

We had a great time looking at all the animals, and Lorcan loved them all, but he made a special connection with a certain sea creature.

At the seal pool, I turned around to see him staring intently through the viewing window. A beautiful seal had come right up to the window and stayed there for ages just looking straight into his eyes. He was over the moon and his face was a joy to see – it was lit up with the biggest smile we had ever seen.

On a trip to London, we came across a man dressed up as Darth Vader (of *Star Wars* fame, for those who didn't know that already!). Luke posed with him for a picture, holding a light sabre, and Lorcan, who usually refuses to have a picture taken with anyone in a costume, shot across and grabbed the light sabre. He then proceeded to clash sabres with Darth Vader. The poor guy had to encourage Lorcan to *pretend* to battle rather than bash away and clatter the sabres, but Lorcan was having a great time.

With Mrs Stevens moving up to Year Five, as we saw in Chapter 4, I was still concerned about how Lorcan would get on in Year Two. I needn't have worried. His new teacher, Mrs Carvajal, was amazing. We had a programme that included three sessions a week with one-to-one learning for Lorcan, or with a few other children. Mrs Carvajal put her heart and soul into following that programme and Lorcan began to make astounding progress. The speech-and-language therapist had regular meetings with me and school staff and was always there to answer queries, and it worked superbly.

In fact, Lorcan made such great progress that he actually missed some of the programme steps out, which was remarkable.

Because of our fears that Lorcan was also autistic – a fact of which I had been convinced for years – Dr John had referred me to the Child and Adolescent Mental Health Services (CAMHS), and I was given a form to fill in, which was a list of symptoms of autism, and boxes to tick if my child displayed those traits. I knew which boxes to tick to maximize my chance of getting something done, but I don't wish to cheat the system, so I filled it in honestly. They refused to see my boy and immediately 'closed the case'.

Fuming, I replied with long, fully referenced letter detailing why Lorcan must be seen: he suffers from a severe anxiety disorder; he still has selective mutism in school; he has a sibling with Asperger's syndrome; and so on. The letter ran to four pages – and I had researched it thoroughly, bombarding them with references to recent research about selective mutism and its link to autism.

I wrote,

> According to Craig (1993) 'there is a growing body of research that suggests children with language disorders (selective mutism) often have social skills deficits.' Ford et al. (1998) found 'interpersonal interactions, social/emotional development and academic performance are all areas of concern about a child with selective mutism.'

I pointed out the detrimental effect of his inability to speak to others, on both his learning and his social skills, and I ended it with another quote from recent research: 'There is a need for all professionals, especially CAMHS psychologists, to be better educated about selective mutism and its treatment' (Roe, 2011).

In October, we received a letter from CAMHS offering an appointment the following month. We were to see the consultant clinical psychologist, and, hilariously, when I walked in the room he said, 'I assume your husband wrote this letter?' What a cheek! No he did not! Anyway, he was a very nice man and he agreed that Lorcan had traits of Asperger's and put him on the waiting list for the Neuro-Developmental Pathway, which is a new initiative. It is used for children suspected to be on the autistic spectrum and involves paediatricians, speech therapists, psychiatrists and psychologists, who all keep an eye on the child and work out the best way forward for their development and educational needs.

As I said, very few professionals are trained to deal with selective mutism – or even recognize it – and that included my own GP husband. Unfortunately, he had never heard of the syndrome until we encountered it with Lorcan so, when I noticed a course advertised on the Selective Mutism Information and Research Association (SMIRA) website (smira.org.uk), in nearby Oldham, it caught my attention. It was run by Maggie Johnson, a speech therapist and a leading expert in selective mutism, who wrote the bible for the condition. She began working with children who had been identified with it back in the seventies and now does seminars all over the country.

I would have loved to have attended myself but it was quite expensive, so we decided it would be more sensible for Dave to go, as there is always a chance he will have patients with the same problem.

The course was a full day and he gained a lot of information on selective mutism. It was followed by a question-and-answer session. He found it really useful and brought some written information home for me to gen up on.

Oddly, at the time of writing, he does now have a patient with the condition, which was interesting. The child's mum phoned me and I had a chat with her, but I wonder how many more there are who are literally suffering in silence and are not being recognized.

In April 2012, Lorcan was seen at school by the educational psychologist. Interestingly, Lorcan spoke to her, albeit in a whisper, but he gave some truly bizarre answers to her questions. He was very fidgety but settled when she allowed him to doodle.

As she talked to him, he started to have a good root around in her bag, and, when she asked if he liked her, he made it absolutely clear that he didn't – all the time with an endearing smile, as if butter wouldn't melt!

After making her assessment, she advised that Lorcan should have no problems with learning. But people with Asperger's often misinterpret things they are told at school, or exam questions. It is usually less noticeable in primary school but can be problematic as they get older, especially in answering exam questions in GCSEs and A-levels.

Towards the end of the Christmas holidays, when Lorcan was still in Year Two, he began getting upset and agitated. He kept asking me, 'How many days until school?' Then he started saying, 'I don't want to go back to school,' which was really unlike him.

Then the question became, 'How many days until Wednesday?' But, no matter how much we tried to get it out of him, he wouldn't tell us what was wrong.

After days of trying to get him to explain the problem, and with one day to go until the start of term, he suddenly burst into tears and said, 'I don't want to go to school. I don't want to go swimming!'

Swimming lessons at the school begin in Year Three but Lorcan had got it into his head that, since it would be a new calendar year, he would be moving up a class after the Christmas holidays. I explained that he would move up a class after the long summer holidays, and that seemed to calm him down. However, Lorcan obviously hadn't fully understood because we went through the same distress with him in the Easter holidays.

This is one of my worries: if he is misunderstanding, even when I think we have covered it well and explained it as much as we can, what else does he not understand?

Lorcan's sleeping problems lasted until he was about seven, when we finally got him to sleep in his own bed, and he started sleeping through the night, most of the time. He still had all his cuddly monkeys ranged around him, to protect him overnight and, as an added bonus, Jess had taken to spending the night on the windowsill in his room. Although this was very nice, and was quite a help in getting him willingly to bed in the evening, it wasn't so wonderful in the morning. Like most cats, she is an early riser and took to leaping on Lorcan's bed at the crack of dawn, miaowing for her breakfast, so it was a double-edged sword. But he loved having her in the room with him.

She also developed a fondness for Lorcan's inflatable bed, which he uses when he wants to sleep in Luke's room. We had to buy a new one because she punctured the first.

Jess likes to join us for the bedtime story and I know she doesn't understand, but she always looks as if she were listening.

Lorcan and I recently started reading the Harry Potter series. Lorcan reads the first paragraph, then I continue. It is taking much longer to read the books to Lorcan than it did to Luke, mainly because he likes to interrupt and make comments on what I'm reading, such as telling me that Harry's friend and fellow wizard Hermione Granger is silly for getting upset. He also inter-rupts frequently to laugh hysterically at things in the book he finds funny, such as Aunt Petunia calling her son Dudley Dursley 'Dinky Duddydums'. But Lorcan won't let his dad read because, he tells Dave, 'You don't do the funny voices like Mummy does.'

Mind you, I have started to wonder if I've

overdone my dramatic reading voices when I read to Lorcan. Last week he was reading to me his book *Five on a Treasure Island*, when he started doing the most bizarre voices imaginable. He did a different one for each character, and insisted on renaming the character of Anne, saying, 'I'm calling her Annie.' He is actually really good at doing voices and very funny. When he had finished his dramatic reading, he looked at me and we both burst out laughing!

As I said goodnight, he said, 'Can I read in a funny voice again tomorrow?' This was great to hear as we have serious issues getting Lorcan to do homework, and any schoolwork. He gets furious when he finds something difficult and I have been worried his schoolwork will suffer and he will fall behind. Now he is finding reading easier and doing funny voices he is happier to get his head into a book. I'm not sure he will ever do homework happily though.

At the moment the school say his reading is up to standard – although their standard isn't always my standard. But I don't want to push him or get him tutors because I don't want to put any pressure on him. As long as he learns to read and write and do his sums, he'll be fine.

As he's happy to read to me, I did record him once or twice to let the teachers hear him, but the way they assess him is to get him to point at certain words, to prove he recognizes them. That fills in their assessment forms, but I don't care about their forms, I want him to be able to read to a decent standard.

He'll happily read most of the time, but he won't do schoolwork at home. Luke hated homework but he'd do it; he'd whinge and moan about it for two days first, but he'd do it. Lorcan doesn't want to pick up a pencil. All through the summer holidays, not once did he have a pencil or pen in his hand, and nothing will make him do homework.

Lorcan is really getting into the swing of things with Harry Potter. He came home from school recently with 'I must not tell lies' inked onto his hand – just like Harry in *Harry Potter and the Order of the Phoenix*, when he had a painful punishment inflicted on him with the 'blood quill'. It showed he had been paying attention, which is not obvious at the time, as he often messes about when I am reading, hiding Jess under the bedcovers, wriggling his toes for her to pounce on and generally being silly. He seems unable to sit still for long. He now gets a small toy or something out of my jewellery box to fiddle with while I am reading and that works really well.

Luke has always loved Harry Potter and that has rubbed off on Lorcan. He has watched all the films, over and over, and, in May, for Luke's birthday, we took them to the Studio Tour. He loved the huge spider, Aragog, and Dobby the house elf, but his favourite exhibit was the half-giant Hagrid's motorcycle, as he and Luke were allowed to sit in it.

That same month, we went down to north London, where Dave's brother Mark lives with his wife, Aga, and little daughter, Hanna. Dave's parents were over for a visit along with his sisters, Stephanie and Marie Louise, with her daughter Aine, so we drove down to spend the day with the family. Lorcan had been talking well in school, so all the way there I kept wondering how he would be with them all.

As well as Dave's family, Aga's mother joined us and, because it was a beautiful sunny day, we spent the afternoon in the garden. The two girls were getting on for two at the time and were very sweet and amusing. Lorcan really enjoyed watching his two little cousins playing.

At one point I walked through the lounge and Lorcan's granny was talking to him. She asked him if he was enjoying himself, probably expecting a nod. I was shocked to hear him say, 'Yes!' It was quite quiet but I heard it. Progress!

CHAPTER 8

A STAR IS BORN

One night, in May 2012, I was tossing and turning in bed, unable to sleep, and I decided to get up and kill some time on the computer. I'm quite a fan of social networking, so I was flicking between Twitter and Facebook and I then flicked onto the website of the cat charity the Scratching Post (scratchingpost.co.uk) and an advert caught my eye.

The charity Cats Protection (cats.org.uk) – who were known as the Cats Protection League till 1998 – were looking for nominees for the National Cat of the Year Awards. There were five different categories and they wanted to know about pets who had helped their owners or other humans, either in a heroic way or in everyday behaviour. When I saw the Best Friends category, I immediately thought of Jessi-cat and Lorcan, so I wrote an email saying that Lorcan has selective mutism and how much Jess helps him.

Jess was already a beauty queen. In November, she had been voted 'Dreamies Deputy' for the Northwest in a poll on the *Treats for Cats* Facebook page, sponsored by cat treat manufacturer Dreamies.

As a prize, she received a framed picture and a boxful of cat toys and treats. Plus, her picture featured in their 2012 calendar.

But this competition was about much more than being a calendar girl.

The next day I read some of the other submissions – all very elaborate accounts of cats doing marvellous things. There was one who had scared off a burglar, another who had saved her owner from a diabetic coma and a one-eyed rescue cat who had become a movie star. Jess didn't stand a chance against these fantastic felines and I assumed Cats Protection would want a rescue moggy rather than a pedigree.

Even so, after a few weeks I received a phone call from a lady at Cats Protection saying they really loved our story and they wanted to hear more. Jessi-cat was being put forward to the judges to see if she was in the final for her category, and she asked if I would be prepared to participate in 'reasonable publicity'.

'Yes, OK,' I said, without stopping to consider what that meant.

'Would you be prepared to come down to London for the awards ceremony if Jess gets through?' she asked.

'Yes, of course I would,' I said merrily, all the time thinking we had a snowball's chance in hell of her getting into the final.

Soon after that, we went off to Anglesey for a few days and had a wonderful family time, so I forgot all about the awards. On our return, in mid-June, I opened my inbox to find an email that said they had been trying to contact me. Jess had made the finals!

I was in complete shock as I didn't really expect to get that far, but it was exciting news.

The charity prepared a press release and then began arranging for a photographer to come and take some pictures, as well as a camera crew to film Lorcan and the cat in action and an interview with me, for their website. We arranged the filming for Wednesday, 27 June, and then I took a phone call the next day arranging for the photographer to come – he couldn't do Wednesday but could do Friday.

Like a total fool, I hadn't read the emails properly and, as a result of the call, I thought the *whole thing* had been changed to Friday. So, when Wednesday came around, I went to the supermarket and then went out shopping for some material to cover my dining chairs. When I got home I hung some curtains and was about to start cutting up material for my chair covers but stopped for a quick sandwich.

At that point I noticed that a big four-by-four had been parked outside for ages but I carried on with my lunch and switched the computer on to check my emails. I nearly died when the first one popped up with 'Today's filming' in the subject line. The crew had been sitting outside all this time and I had about half an hour to tidy up the mess I'd made, get Lorcan from school and tidy myself up before being on camera.

I rushed outside to speak to them and explained that I thought they were coming on Friday instead. Luckily, the crew were really lovely and said there was no rush, but by then I was in full panic mode. Looking back, I realize that my frantic dash was probably for the best, because I was so busy dragging the vacuum cleaner round the house, throwing shopping bags in random cupboards, looking for Jessi and slapping some lipstick on that there was no time to be anxious.

Lorcan and Jess really enjoyed the filming – and the crew had thoughtfully bought sweets for the boys, which no doubt helped. Jess kept sneaking around, sniffing cameras and rubbing her head on equipment. Lorcan was silent but very smiley and obviously enjoyed showing Jess off.

Fascinated with interesting technology, as usual, he fiddled with various bits of equipment, and the very patient cameraman let Lorcan switch the camera off and on. He also asked Lorcan to do a thumbs-up if I did well in the interview. He loved that.

Two days later a photographer came. Jessi posed beautifully for her pictures and Lorcan beamed at him, and seemed to enjoy the experience. Lorcan picked up a camera lens and nearly gave the photographer a heart attack.

'Give that back, Lorcan,' I said. 'It's probably worth about five thousand pounds!' The photographer, who had turned a little pale, took it back gratefully and stashed it safely away.

In July, ITV Granada (it used to be known as Granada Television) saw the press release and wanted to film us as well. I was totally terrified. The filming for Cats Protection had been stressful enough but this would be on TV for all our family, friends and neighbours to see.

Despite my jitters, I agreed to do it and had a phone call from the Granada presenter Paul Crone, who was coming to film the piece. Paul has been with Granada since 1984, and for more than twenty years has been one of the company's most familiar faces. During this time he's raised more than half a million pounds with various charity appeals.

I was concerned that Paul's visit might make Lorcan anxious, but I needn't have worried: he had an amazing time. Paul is so good with children that he relaxed Lorcan and immediately put him at his ease, chatting away to him. Lorcan didn't speak to Paul but he helped to work the camera and he cheekily pilfered one of Paul's key rings without our noticing.

Lorcan was filmed cuddling and playing with Jess on the floor and Paul made Lorcan giggle like mad by tickling his feet and telling him they were 'whiffy'. Lorcan is football mad and Paul even had a kickabout in the garden with him. When he said, 'Kick the ball at me,' Lorcan did just that – a belter of a shot straight at his head. Twice!

On the Monday before the awards, we were asked to do an interview for BBC Radio Manchester on Becky Want's show. The cat came with us but wasn't up for performing and refused to miaow on air. Lorcan was equally unvocal but took delight in pulling faces at me to make me laugh during the interview as well as squeaking his chair loudly, so at least he made his presence felt.

The Cat of the Year awards, we were told, would be held at the Savoy hotel in London on 16 August. On the big day, Lorcan and I were up early and got ready in plenty of time. I think Luke might have liked to come but he is so understanding when it comes to Lorcan, and he knew the awards ceremony was his brother's time in the spotlight, so he didn't say anything about coming. Luke would get his little moment the next day, when I took them both to the TV studios for an interview and he got to speak on camera.

We were booked on the train at nine in the morning, and at Manchester Piccadilly we collected the tickets and everything went like clockwork. I took my iPad, so Lorcan kept himself occupied on the journey, playing games. By the time we got to London, I was really looking forward to the meal at the Savoy but Lorcan is such a fussy eater that I knew he would hardly touch it so, at Euston Station, I bought him a Burger King, then we got a cab straight to the hotel. We were due at 12.30 p.m. and our timing was perfect.

The hotel was beautiful. We had been told to go to the river entrance, which is on the Thames, so that we didn't have to negotiate our way through the lobby and restaurants. There was someone at the door to greet us, and they gave us a programme and directed us upstairs to get our badges, then we were led into a beautiful reception room with burgundy and cream walls, gold chandeliers and thick plush carpets. There were groups of people standing around chatting and waiters were bringing round champagne and wine on trays.

A huge board at one side of the room proclaimed, 'Meet the Finalists' and below the heading were blown-up photos of all the cats and their owners. Lorcan was beaming when he saw the picture of Jess, with a little blurb about their relationship. The chief executive of Cats Protection, Peter Hepburn, came over to introduce himself and had a chat, before circulating to the other owners.

We also met the ladies who run *Scratching Post*, the website where we had seen the initial advert for the award entries. They were really lovely and friendly. A photographer was wandering around taking pictures of everyone and cheeky

Lorcan hid behind a curtain and peeped out at her.

After half an hour of mingling we went downstairs into a big function room, where tables were laid out for the meal with crisp white tablecloths and silver cutlery, and there was a stage at one end. It was absolutely beautiful, very grand. Lorcan being Lorcan, he took it all in his stride and wasn't impressed at all. If it had been Luke, he'd have been jumping up and down with excitement and I thought it was a really wonderful occasion. The food was lovely, a delicious three-course meal but, as predicted, Lorcan didn't eat any of it – except for the dessert, which was ice cream.

We didn't know anyone on our table at the ceremony but I was chatting away to my fellow guests, particularly one very friendly man who said, 'I think you're going to win this.' Of course, I said, 'Don't be daft.' Then he turned to Lorcan and said, 'What's that you're drinking?'

Very, very quietly he said, 'Apple juice.' I was amazed he had spoken to a complete stranger, as he would normally have smiled but stayed silent. It was wonderful to hear, but I was far too anxious and thinking, Oh God! What if I have to say something?

To be honest, for that reason, the whole ceremony is a bit of a blur. I was so wound up and anxious in case we had to go on the stage, and worried I would have to speak, that I was finding it quite stressful.

The comedian Ed Byrne, the newsreader Jan Leeming and the model Lucy Pinder were among the presenters there and the master of ceremonies was Alan Dedicoat, the famous voiceover man from *Strictly Come Dancing* and *The National Lottery: In It To Win It*, so his voice was very familiar, even though his face wasn't.

The first category to be announced was ours, the Best Friends. Alan told the audience the gong was 'for those animals who have shown a remarkable bond with their owners'.

He added, 'Cats have an amazing ability, as we know, to help people, whether it be building confidence, recovering from illness or just easing loneliness and depression.'

Then he introduced Rick Wakeman, who walked up on stage and started talking about the winner. As I listened I began to think, Ooh it might be us. But it still came as a jolt when he announced, 'Ladies and gentleman, the winner is Jessi-cat.' As the picture of Jess flashed up on a big screen behind him, there was an audible wave of 'aah' from the cat lovers in the audience.

Rick carried on with a speech about Jess, and his assessment of this little creature's impact on our lives hit the nail squarely on the head.

'All three cats have been a huge support to their owners, but Jessi-cat is my winner,' he explained. 'The bond between Jessi-cat and Lorcan is incredible and it has clearly had a hugely positive impact on Lorcan's home and school life. Jessi-cat helps Lorcan to communicate and express emotions that ordinarily Lorcan wouldn't be able to do.'

Lorcan's reaction was very calm. He didn't jump up and down or make a sound: he just stood up, put his backpack on, and followed me up to the stage. I don't know why he felt the need to put his backpack on first – either it made him feel more secure in an unusual situation, like carrying a favourite cuddly toy, or he thought it was all over and we were going home straight after picking up the award.

By the time we got to the stage I was shaking like a leaf. Lorcan was absolutely fine. Rick handed me this heavy glass trophy and I said, 'Do I have to do anything?'

'No, it's fine,' he answered, smiling, which put me at ease a bit. We didn't have to speak, which was a huge relief because I was terrified. Lorcan seemed quite happy, posing for photos with Rick and me, backpack firmly fixed to his back and beaming broadly at everyone.

After we returned to our table Lucy Pinder presented the Bravery Award to a cat called Charley, who had raised the alarm when her diabetic owner collapsed in the middle of the night. Then Ed Byrne presented the Most Incredible Story Award to a moggy who survived a horrific dog attack and lost a leg. Next up was Jan Leeming, who presented the Outstanding Rescue Cat Award to the owner of Phoenix, who had suffered horrific burns as a kitten and battled through.

During Jan's long and eloquent speech, I noticed a man smiling in our direction. I glanced round to see my seven-year-old son gurning at the newsreader with the most hideous expressions. Clearly he was beginning to get a bit fidgety.

After the prize for Celebrity Cat was handed to Simon Tofield, for his animated character Simon's Cat, who features in the series of the same name, it was time for the overall winner.

Chief executive Peter Hepburn announced, 'This year's Cat of the Year is . . .' – there was a long pause, or should I say paws? – 'Jessi-cat.' Then he gave a little cheer and asked us back onto the stage. I was stunned. It was a big enough shock to win the first one and, when they announced Jessi-cat for the final prize, we just couldn't believe it.

This time Lorcan was a bit braver and dashed up ahead of me, and he took the star-shaped glass trophy when it was offered to him. He stood on the stage, and he smiled for the photos.

Ceremony over, we were directed out of the room to have pictures taken with the awards and with the presenters, and I was interviewed on camera. Lorcan behaved like a little model, posing and smiling on cue. For my part I couldn't help thinking it felt a bit surreal and quite bizarre to find ourselves in this situation because of a cat, but it was fantastic for Lorcan because he loves Jess and it was a great day for him.

After the ceremony, Simon Tofield and his wife Zoe came over to congratulate us and sat with us for a while. Simon was very sweet to Lorcan and drew him a picture of his famous cat in his notebook, which was brilliant, and then signed it. They asked Lorcan when his birthday was and said he had a book coming out in September. Then Zoe took Lorcan's address. The following month, a lovely hand-drawn birthday card arrived for Lorcan's birthday with a wonderful picture of Jess on it, from Simon and Zoe. Lorcan was thrilled! He's made me cover it in protective plastic.

A few weeks later the new book arrived for Lorcan with a picture Simon had drawn of Simon's Cat and Jess, also signed. Lorcan loves the book. He looks at it a lot and always finds something new to see. He laughs hysterically at some of the pictures and really enjoys it.

The train going home was at peak time and really, really expensive, but I splashed out and booked first class because I thought that if Lorcan was tired there would be a bit more room. We were pretty loaded up because we had been showered with gifts all afternoon. There were the two heavy glass trophies, which had been put in boxes, a framed photo of Jess, a big box of flowers, loads of cat toys and three months' supply of cat litter from the ceremony's sponsor, Verdo, plus some cat food. I also had my big bag with a cardigan, iPad and snacks for Lorcan, so we were loaded down. Lorcan was carrying two little Cats Protection bags through the station and my flowers, and when we got there we crawled up the stairs to the first-class lounge, just so we could sit somewhere. There was nowhere to sit in the noisy area so we had to sit in the quiet area. Having been quiet all day Lorcan was itching to run about and make some noise, and I kept having to say, 'Shh! Shh!' In the end I gave up and we left and walked outside the station. It was a lovely day, so Lorcan ran around until it was time to get on the train.

By now it was seven o'clock on a Thursday evening, so the train was full of businessmen and -women. We got chatting to a really nice man sitting with us and he asked all about the awards ceremony and Lorcan was talking away to me, chuffed to bits, but he wouldn't answer the chap directly.

By the time we got home it was really late – after 10 p.m. – so we had time only for a quick bath and then it was straight to bed. But first, naturally, Lorcan had to tell Jessi-cat she'd won. He broke the news in a very matter-of-fact way, but he put his face right up to her and with a big smile he said, 'You've won Jessi, you've won.' He then arranged the two awards and all the prizes we'd brought back around her on the table where she was sitting and then showed her the cat toys.

Reflecting on that special day, I see that it seems to mark another turning point for Lorcan. I have since come to believe that the awards, going down to London and being on the train must have had a positive effect and the moment that Lorcan quietly replied to the man who asked him what he was drinking keeps flooding back. Things seemed to have steadily improved since. I don't know who he was – he could have been famous, for all I know – but I'm so glad we got chatting to him that day!

CHAPTER 9

FELINE FAME

As we travelled back from the awards on the train I had a phone call from the BBC, asking us to appear on *Breakfast* the following morning. We were already due to do an interview on BBC Radio 5 Live, but, as both were based in Media City, in Salford, it tied in quite well, so I happily agreed. They asked if I could bring Jess, so I said I could but I needed a room where I could get her out of the carrier, as we were going to be there a while.

As it was the summer holidays and I had left Luke behind the day before, while we went to London, I insisted that I be allowed to take him along with me for the interviews. I thought he'd enjoy the experience, but it wasn't just for his sake I wanted him with us. Lorcan is either as good as gold or a holy terror, and Luke often distracts him and stops him getting into mischief.

We had to be up at the crack of dawn to be at the so-called MediaCityUK – the huge development in Salford where the BBC, among others, has some of its operations – for 7.30 the next morning and, after our journey from London and very late night, it was a struggle to get Lorcan up. We finally dragged him out of bed, got him dressed, put Jess in her carrier and set off. It's just as well I have a good hairdresser because there was no time to wash my hair and, thanks to her, it still looked good from when she had styled it two days before.

Dave was driving us to MediaCityUK, but we got a bit lost and ended up being a little late. It was touch and go as to whether we were going to be there in time for the radio show but we just made it and the producer sent us straight in as soon as we arrived. Both boys got to sit in front of a microphone with earphones on, which was an exciting experience for them. Lorcan didn't speak during the interview and when it was over we were left to sit there a little longer, while someone read the news and another reporter did the sports news. It was a fantastic opportunity for the boys to see how a radio station worked and both of them seemed to be having a wonderful time.

After the news, we were ushered out to the green room to wait for our cue for *Breakfast*. We made sure the door was shut, then let Jess out of her carrier for a wander.

The room was furnished with comfy chairs and a TV, where we could watch the show live as it came from the studio next door. On a table in the middle of the room were drinks – tea and coffee – as well as fruit and croissants, so the boys had some breakfast while Jess explored the room. She managed to climb up onto a high windowsill and was quite content looking out at the view. Most of the time, we had the green room to ourselves, although a few people came in for a short while. Nobody minded Jess wandering about and they seemed to like her. One man even asked if he could take a picture of her because his girlfriend loved cats and he thought she was beautiful.

Despite the lovely spread, I couldn't eat breakfast, as I was really nervous about the interview. I'd never been in a TV studio before and I imagined it to be full of dozens of people.

In contrast to his silence in the studio, Lorcan chatted away throughout, and didn't even stop when a couple of strangers came in. When Jess wandered towards the door at one point, he grinned menacingly at me and put his hand on the door handle, as if he was going to let her out. The little terror had heard me saying we needed to watch she didn't slink out when someone opened the door, or she would be running amok in the studios.

After a time we were directed to makeup, so we put Jess back in her box. Lorcan had to sit on a chair and have a brush swished across his face but, amazingly, he didn't object. Luke wasn't supposed to be going on with us, so he didn't have any makeup applied.

When we were finished in makeup we were directed to seats outside the studio, as we were on next. I was racked with nerves by this point and

Lorcan was really quiet. He whispered a little to Luke, but there was no proper talking.

Then came the call – we were on. I got Jess out of the carrier and carried her in and I insisted Luke come in to watch, as I didn't want to leave him in the green room. I couldn't believe how small the studio was. There was just one big red sofa where the presenters, Charlie Stayt and Louise Minchin sat, plus one cameraman and the producer. Charlie and Louise waved us over and Lorcan and I went to sit down. Charlie saw Luke standing near the door and said, 'Who's that? Come on over here.' So Luke joined us on the sofa, too. I thought it was really kind of him and fantastic for Luke. Luke is a lovely, selfless boy who often puts Lorcan's needs before his own, so it was great that he got to take part.

At the beginning of the interview I was talking while simultaneously trying to keep hold of Jess, who was attempting to escape the sofa, as well as keeping an eye on Lorcan, who was a bit trouble-some after we'd been in the green room for a while. It wasn't the most relaxing of starts to an interview.

Charlie asked Luke what difference the cat had made to his brother and, because he was totally unprepared and hadn't been expecting to speak, he answered really naturally.

He said, 'He talks to his teacher more than he used to and he talks to his friends more.' He would definitely have been nervous if he'd had advance warning that he was going to be asked a question, but he did really well and spoke very clearly.

Charlie then asked Lorcan how you talk to a cat, but Lorcan didn't speak. He just bent down with his mouth to Jessi-cat's ear, as if he were whispering to her, although that's not how he speaks to her at home at all. He kept peering at a huge picture of himself and Jessi on one of the screens in the studio and we could see him looking at that when we played the video back later. Charlie was very sweet when he was trying to get Lorcan to talk, and mentioned that he had heard him chatting away earlier, but I knew he wouldn't respond, because he'd stopped talking properly when we left the green room.

After the interview, we stayed there for a few minutes talking to Louise and Charlie. They had a good look at Jess and were both lovely, but Lorcan still didn't say a word.

I'm not sure whether Jess enjoyed her moment in the limelight, but I think she did. She gave me a little bite while we were on the sofa, which she does occasionally anyway, then licks the skin afterwards. It is known as the Birman nip. It doesn't hurt and never leaves a mark and it is thought by many to be a sign of affection.

All things considered, it went surprisingly well.

After leaving the studio, we were outside putting Jessi back in her box when I noticed the former goalkeeper Peter Schmeichel – known chiefly for his years at Manchester United – going in after us, so I pointed him out to the boys, who were chuffed to bits.

We were then free to go and, as we climbed in the taxi to go home, I heaved a huge sigh of relief. Both boys were chatting away about the radio and the TV interview afterwards. Luke said it was 'awesome' and Lorcan said it was 'my best day ever. Except from when Jessi won her awards!'

I asked Lorcan if he'd like to go on TV again. He said he definitely would.

It was a nerve-racking experience but it was worth it to get a little more awareness of selective mutism. Most people haven't heard of it and soon after the show, a woman contacted the selective mutism Facebook page and said, 'I saw that little boy and I thought, That's my child. I think my son had selective mutism.' It was nice to know we had helped her, and maybe some others along the way.

After the awards and the TV interviews, Jess's fame spread far and wide. She even featured in a magazine in Spain and, with all the publicity we were getting, the Cats Protection video was proving hugely popular on the Internet, with more than 130,000 hits.

I decided to give Jess her own Twitter account. At the time of writing, she has more than a thousand followers and she tweets about mischief she gets up to, how she winds up the dog and all sorts of catty little comments. She also tweets cute little pictures of herself, which cat-loving followers enjoy looking at, and sometimes her furry friends tweet pictures of themselves too, but there is also a serious side. Twitter allows another platform for supporting autism and selective-mutism causes, while having fun at the same time.

Jess's win was reported in the papers and in some cat magazines as well. A few days afterwards, I was contacted by the Birman Cat Club, who have now made Lorcan an honorary member. They asked if we could write an article about the Cat of the Year Awards for them, so Adam wrote a piece, which appeared in their winter magazine and which you can see as the appendix of this book on page 209.

The headline was, 'Fame for Jessi-cat and Lorcan', and it was a really thoughtfully written article, all about his mutism and how his love for Jess has improved his life, both at home and school. 'Lorcan is making huge improvements and showing that, with the right help, children with selective mutism can excel and even overcome their anxiety eventually,' he wrote.

He ended the piece with a heart-warming tribute to the family pet: 'Jessi-cat shows just how much a cat can change a person's life – no matter how old they are!'

Along with the article, the magazine printed a lovely letter from Jess's breeder, Janet. 'Jessi really has found a wonderful home and, if you read all the reports, she has made a lifelong companion in Lorcan,' she wrote. 'This wonderful special boy has obviously gained the love and respect of this Birman.'

In September 2012, Luke was leaving primary school to go up to secondary school. As any parent knows, choosing the right secondary for your child is a stressful business and whatever you decide will affect the rest of his or her life. When it came to Luke we found the local schools highly unsuitable, for one reason or another, but we visited Knutsford Academy, about twenty miles away from us, and loved everything about it.

As well as worrying about Luke, I was really concerned about the effect his move would have on his little brother. My biggest worry was that if someone was mean to Lorcan, he could always have told Luke and I felt it was less likely he would be picked on at school as long he had an older brother there. But he has George and the other boys in the class and, so far, there have been no problems with bullying. It's a tiny school, with small classes, and there are only about two hundred kids in the entire school, so it has been a happy environment for Lorcan.

After the awards ceremony, Lorcan's speech continued to improve. We had seen Dr Anthony John, the paediatrician who deals with autism in our area, again in February and, as he was concerned about possible Asperger's, he had advised the Child and Adolescent Mental Health Services (CAMHS) they might have to look out of area if Lorcan's needs could not be met in Trafford. This led us to an autism specialist, Mali Rashidi, who is also a speech therapist. Dr John wanted Mali's input because her specialism in the field meant that she would look for different things that may be too subtle for other professionals to pick up.

In July, Mali came and watched Lorcan at school, and a month later, during the summer holidays, she came to see me at home, when the children were out. She was very thorough, asking me lots of questions about what he was like as a baby, what he used to do and how he behaves and speaks now. She said she thought it was Asperger's but she believed he was coping with it on a day-to-day basis because we, as a family, had been through it before and have learned to adapt our behaviour.

As parents, you know when your child is not being deliberately naughty, that he can't help behaving in a certain way, so he's not going to get screamed at. She thought Lorcan was doing well because of the way we dealt with it, which was good to hear.

Dave has to take a lot of credit because he is very easygoing and takes things as they come. Although Adam isn't his actual son, he has always treated him as if he were, and has the perfect nature to deal with all three boys. We both tend just to get on with it and deal with it, but, if he were a different kind of person, with a less even temper, it could have been difficult, because it does sometimes seem as if Lorcan is just being naughty. I know he's not, because I know what's going on in his head and there will be something that he hasn't understood, and I know he gets upset when he doesn't know what's going on.

Luckily, Dave is mild-mannered, quiet and very laid back, so we mosey along together and everything's fine.

Mali also suggested the selective mutism was 'comorbid', or, in layman's terms, existing alongside the Asperger's but not actually connected to it. As a result of her assessment, we got an appointment to see a child psychiatrist at CAMHS in October.

Before we went, the psychiatrist, Dr Sharma, rang me and he told me to come in myself, but asked me not to bring Lorcan, which I thought was odd. Then he asked, 'Is your husband coming with you?' I didn't think about it. I just replied, 'He can't, he's at work.' But something about the question set alarm bells ringing, so, when I spoke to my mum, she volunteered to come with me.

Mali Rashidi was with Dr Sharma when we were shown into his office. First they went over various things to check whether he had signs of obsessive-compulsive disorder, and they concluded that he didn't. We had wondered, because he likes things done a certain way and he does have a tendency to develop obsessions.

His latest big thing is the British entertainment duo Ant and Dec. He is a superfan. He records all the screenings of their show *Saturday Night Takeaway* and watches them over and over. He particularly enjoys the slot in the programme known as 'The End of the Show Show', in which Ant and Dec perform with a celebrity guest at the conclusion of each show. Lorcan especially likes the one in which Ant and Dec performed 'Let's Get Ready to Rhumble'. He even got me to fill in a YouGov survey on Ant and Dec and, when asked which three words he would use to describe the show, he immediately chose 'cool', 'awesome' and 'epic'. He also said it was 'ingenious'.

It's lovely to see him watching Ant and Dec. He is totally focused on what is going on and screams with delighted laughter. He also pauses the TV and rewinds it if he spots Ant and Dec, even in an advert. He recently acquired a 'Dec' cardboard face mask, which terrifies the dog, but Lorcan loves it. He puts it in his bedroom window facing out at night, which must look a bit creepy to the neighbours.

Anyway, the fact that he didn't have obsessive-compulsive disorder was a relief. They then explained the reason they hadn't wanted to see Lorcan at that appointment. They said there was a test named ADOS – the Autism Diagnostic Observation Schedule – in which they play games with the children and instigate communication. They're looking for certain reactions to what they say and do, but Dr Sharma said they would get a false result because of the selective mutism.

Instead, they had watched the clip from the BBC *Breakfast* interview and listened to my concerns. Then they gave the diagnosis. My gorgeous little boy had Asperger's syndrome.

Because I had another son with Asperger's, I had obviously known, in my heart of hearts, for years. But, as a mother, having seen the horrible things Adam had been through, I suppose part of me was hoping that I was wrong. Also, as Adam was quite old at diagnosis, I expected Lorcan to be in the system for years, possibly getting the diagnosis at fifteen or older.

When my worst suspicions were confirmed it took a minute for it to sink in, then I broke down and sobbed. I was devastated. I was crying for Lorcan's future, for the ignorance he will possibly face, for the battles I know were ahead of us. He's my baby boy. A gorgeous, smiley, mischievous menace. I thought of all the problems he might face at secondary school and for the rest of his life, and it felt as if someone had squeezed all the breath out of me. I had done my fighting for Adam, and now I was going into battle again.

After that, the only thing I remember was asking, 'When do I tell him?' They advised that it is best if children are made aware by the time they go to secondary school, then we were given an information pack from the National Autistic Society and we left.

I was so glad my mum had come along with me, as I really needed the love and support at that moment. After we left the office, I turned to Mum and asked, 'What did they say?' I was in such a state of shock that I couldn't actually remember whether they had said autism or Asperger's. I remember thinking, Oh, my God! They've given me the diagnosis now. But I didn't know what the diagnosis was.

It shouldn't have come as a huge shock but, even

though you've known yourself for years, until it becomes official there's always a little hope in the back of your mind that you're wrong, that he doesn't have autism and everything's going to be great.

Up to that point there had been things that I had been aware of and, while I wasn't actually ignoring them, I wasn't dealing with them until I had a diagnosis.

I was upset for only five minutes. It was just a knee-jerk reaction. There was no feeling of relief, initially, but there was later, when I thought, Right, I've got a job to do. I'm going get on and do it.

Having seen what Adam went through I was not going to let it happen to another child of mine and, because of him, the school have taken me seriously pretty much since the word go. Adam had been one of their brightest, always top of the class, a star pupil, brilliant and quite confident – and even had poems published in primary school. Yet they watched him go through the mill, and the problems he faced, so they know that I know what I'm talking about and they listen when I talk to them.

Apart from that moment at Dr Sharma's office, I haven't shed a tear over Lorcan's condition because I need to keep a clear head to deal with it. I don't have a job but I do work, because all day my table has got papers scattered over it, and there's always someone I have to contact, or something I have to get done for somebody. It's not going to help if I feel sorry for myself. It's not about me. They're my kids and I've got to fight for them to have the best life that they can. That's my job.

When Dave got home that night I told him what Mali and Dr Sharma had said, and he said that was what he had thought all along. Adam had spotted the signs of Asperger's when Lorcan was small, so he wasn't surprised, either. Then I had to tell Luke. I sat him down and explained very simply what Asperger's meant and I showed him some cartoons explaining it. He took it all in and understood really quickly.

'Could I have it too?' he asked. 'As both my brothers have it?' I reassured Luke that we were quite sure he didn't, and we showed him a video on YouTube explaining very simply what Asperger's syndrome is.

I hadn't decided when to tell Lorcan about it. I wanted to wait until I had the letter confirming the diagnosis, but I had no idea that it would take months to arrive. As a mum, I felt I needed that piece of paper to begin to accept the diagnosis, so it's really important that these letters get out to parents really quickly. I remember asking my mum over and over if they had definitely given the diagnosis because I felt that without that piece of paper there was no proof, that maybe we'd heard it wrong. Plus, I needed to tell Lorcan but I couldn't tell him until I had the diagnosis in black and white.

We received the actual diagnosis in early October and we finally received the letter some three months later. In the meantime, I made numerous phone calls to CAMHS to ask where it was; it got to the point where they knew who I was when I rang. After weeks and weeks of this, I started to get really annoyed. After one call, I had just put the phone down and started formulating a scathing letter of complaint when the phone rang. It was a really helpful lady from the National Autistic Society. I explained to her what had happened, she rang CAMHS and, lo and behold, the letter arrived after a few days.

I remember watching a programme years ago about a young boy with Asperger's. He said he had always known he was different, but he didn't know why. I didn't want Lorcan feeling like that and I didn't want him to be told when he was older and for it to be a huge shock. I also didn't want to force the issue, but I knew when the right opportunity arose I would tell him what the doctors had said.

In the end I actually got quite anxious about it, and kept putting it off, as I wasn't sure how he would react. Then the perfect moment came around.

We were sitting reading together and we started talking about how some people are 'different'. My heart was hammering but I carried along that route, knowing the time had come. Lorcan was talking about people like Harry Potter's fellow student Neville Longbottom, who, like Harry, is in Gryffindor House at Hogwarts and is different from the other boys, and I was also explaining why we mustn't point and comment loudly on people in the street. Lorcan nodded sagely and said, 'Some people pick their nose and some people might have funny hair.' I briefly explained what Asperger's is. He thought about it and said, 'I'm happy this way,' which brought a lump to my throat. I made a big thing of telling him about famous people with Asperger's, such as Microsoft co-founder Bill Gates and the seventeenth-century physicist and mathematician Isaac Newton, and I think that distracted him.

Adam gave him a book called *All Cats Have Asperger Syndrome* by Kathy Hoopmann, which was perfect. It explains really simply and nicely all the different aspects of Asperger's – such as over-sensitive hearing, running away from being touched and having very particular eating habits – through the behaviour of cats. It includes lots of lovely pictures of cats, which Lorcan loved looking at. He did turn the page rapidly if it was something he didn't like, or didn't want to think about, such

150

as the Asperger's cat who struggled to make friends. I'm still not sure how much Lorcan understands about Asperger's syndrome, as he is still very young. I just don't want it to be a huge shock when he is older. He accepts himself as he is and is happy with who he is, which is great.

Later, when we went downstairs, Lorcan made a beeline for Jessi and made a huge fuss of her. Then he told her, 'Hello Jessi, you have Asperger's! Did you know?' I think he found it much easier to understand what Asperger's is from looking at the cats and, again, it gave him another link with Jessi. Watching him talking to Jess about it, I felt a huge sense of relief that I'd told him, as I had been worried about how he would take it.

Since that day we have hardly discussed Asperger's syndrome. I think it is enough that he knows he has it and, if he has any questions, I hope he will ask me. Because Lorcan has two communication disorders and struggles to express his emotions, I have always tried to bring him up to ask me anything he doesn't understand. He is doing well with that and will ask me lots of questions all the time, but they are rarely to do with him personally and are never about emotions, as he still struggles with them. They are usually really quirky, unusual questions like, 'Who was the first person to be the first person ever to walk this land?' Or, 'Where did all the water in the world come from?'

A recent enquiry was, 'If England is not very big, why don't we expand it?'

His curiosity is really endearing but the questions are always fact-based and he never raises the subject of either the mutism or the Asperger's syndrome.

As I have now discovered, lots of people with Asperger's have cats. Animals are a common help but cats seem to provide a special comfort. There are a couple of people with Asperger's whom we talk to on Twitter and one – Kevin Healey, who runs a huge campaign against autism bullying – recently sent us a picture of his beautiful moggy. It was a Birman, and looked just like Jess.

Although Lorcan was still in Year Three when he was diagnosed, and had another three years of primary school, I wanted to make sure we were fully prepared for the challenges he would face when he left. After days of trawling the Internet for more information and advice, I finally went straight to Adam and said, 'I need to know what problems Lorcan's going to face at secondary. Can you help me?'

Adam had been to a local grammar school, and I knew he would tell me the pitfalls at school, but

I wasn't prepared for the long list he eventually handed me, detailing the things that had happened to him. Reading it broke my heart. I had no idea of all the pain and anguish that he had been putting up with on a day-to-day basis, and I was shocked that, throughout his whole time there, and numerous parents' evenings, the teachers had never said a word to me about this.

As well as his experiences, Adam laid out some advice that he felt the teachers could follow to make Lorcan cope more easily with life at school:

- Make sure Lorcan knows exactly what is expected if instructions aren't clear, e.g. do they want note taking or should it be a proper essay?

- Praise his achievements and recognize what he does well as well as pointing out mistakes. Otherwise it will completely knock his confidence; he won't see the point in trying so will give up and fail.

- Group work – quiet children generally get ignored. Put Lorcan with other quiet children. Let him do note taking or put him with a friend he's confident to speak up with. Note taking is good, as his points will be heard regardless of his ability to interrupt, speak up, etc.

- Make sure he knows where he's going or has someone to show him. Needs to be ongoing. Do not stop support if he seems to be coping. Give advance warning of any room changes or unusual lesson activity, e.g. group work, practicals, so he can prepare himself.

- Let him choose where to sit in class if possible.

- Be very clear about what he has to do, e.g. bullet points, paragraph, essay; do not be vague and just leave him to get on with it. Do not assume what you want him to do is obvious if you haven't explicitly told him.

- Asperger's children can get overstimulated, can't filter out background noise, and breaks in big noisy environments like a canteen can be difficult. Asperger's children need somewhere quiet to sit to eat lunch.

- Make sure he is fully prepared for days that are different, e.g. school trips and own-clothes day.

- Teachers need to know that reading aloud may be a problem for Lorcan, especially if his selective mutism continues through secondary school.

- Following practicals in science and other subjects is very difficult, because of literal interpretation, and Lorcan may be unable to ask for help.

Adam obviously went through some huge things at school and, sadly, nobody spotted it. His late diagnosis meant he went through so many night-mares, and nothing can top that. With Lorcan, at least we know early, so we can take this on from a practical perspective.

Because it's not severe autism, but high-functioning Asperger's, I think he has a chance if he gets the right help, so I'm constantly on the Internet, writing emails or phoning, trying to get the best for him. You hear the words 'early inter-vention' over and over again, but where is it? What is being done? I can do all the things I need to do, explain things and make sure he is fine, but he is in school most of his life. That's why I was determined to get him statemented before he goes to secondary school. I thought, OK, he doesn't need it now because the staff at the primary school are brilliant. But what about secondary?

He is already struggling when it comes to understanding some instructions. We have had a few occasions, even in Year Three, when he gets distressed simply because he has maths homework and doesn't understand what he's supposed to do. Consequently, it doesn't get done. How much worse will that be when he gets the volume of homework they get at secondary school?

If I've got to fight for this, and go to a tribunal or through the courts – which I am prepared to do – it's going to take years, so I need to start now.

Having requested a statutory assessment for Lorcan for the second time, I was given a form to fill in. Under the question, 'What are your worries?' there was a tiny box to fill in. Believe me, my worries were a lot bigger than that space would allow me to elaborate! Instead of filling it in, I started writing a potted history of the problems Lorcan has had, and why I want him statemented. In the end, it ran to several pages, so I guess they got a lot more than they bargained for.

Even so, I recently received a letter from our local education authority saying they do not have 'enough evidence at present', so they have decided to defer the decision. My blood is boiling even as I think about it.

Throughout all this, Mali Rashidi was a great help. As an autism specialist who is also a speech-and-language specialist, she possesses a knowledge of autism that astounds me. She is an amazing lady.

Soon after the diagnosis, she invited me to a 'Social Stories Workshop', so I went along to find out what it was all about. The idea is that you write down everything that's going to happen, for your child, so they are not frightened by changes in routine or special events.

For example, when Lorcan had been traumatized by the thought of swimming lessons, the school had done exactly that. They wrote, 'We arrive at the swimming pool. You walk into the changing room, then you change into your swimming trunks. Then walk out to the pool area.' In addition, you can draw pictures, or little stick men, and put photographs in, so they understand what is going on and they can look at it a few times before the event.

Each story is written so that we include plenty of positives and not too many negatives, but it is more complicated than it sounds. When I started the workshop I thought, This'll be easy. Then I got stuck in and thought, Ooh, I think you need a university degree to understand this! It's a formula that you follow to help them get through daunting events and work out their worries. But I have mastered it now, and it really helps him.

Swimming has always been an issue for Lorcan. We have had constant discussions about it and Dave has taken the boys to the local baths on several occasions, but Lorcan has never enjoyed it, and often just sat on the steps of the pool and refused to get in.

The swimming sessions had changed by the time Lorcan started Year Three, which was quite a good thing for us. Instead of going for half an hour every week they were going to do a full hour for six months, from February. This gave us a few months for Lorcan to get used to his new teacher and before being thrown in the deep end – figuratively speaking, of course.

We had talked about it a lot but the subject often upset him, so I was worried. As February approached Lorcan's teacher, Mrs Bernard, raised the matter with the class, and established that there were other children who were nonswimmers and Lorcan wasn't the only one who was scared. Lorcan was as prepared as he could be and I really wanted him to give it a try, and see how he got on. If he was really upset and distressed when he actually went, I would probably have stopped him going.

A few days before the swimming lesson, he was telling me he didn't want to go, but he still couldn't articulate the real reason swimming worried him so much. It could have been change of routine, or unfamiliar venue, and the speech therapist suggested it may be a sensory issue, typical of children with autism, perhaps not liking water on the face or the noise in the swimming baths.

Anyway, he was clearly upset, so I took him to see Mrs Bernard. She asked him what he was scared of and he looked very serious and said, 'Drowning'!

So now we know.

Mrs Bernard was amazing. She patiently explained why that couldn't happen and he seemed much happier.

On the day of the first season I showed him his bag and swimming things and went through the events of the day one more time. He was anxious, but not upset, and off he went.

Afterwards, Mrs Bernard said he did really well. I'm not convinced he will ever learn to swim properly, because he is still not confident in the water, but the fact that he went, and got into the pool without making a huge fuss, is fantastic. Mrs Bernard asked me to take him swimming over the Easter holidays, to boost his confidence, and this time he went happily into the water with Luke.

It still wouldn't be Lorcan's idea of a fun day out, but at least he is no longer terrified, so we'll carry on taking him after the school lessons stop.

The 'drowning' comment is typical of Lorcan, whose imagination often makes him fear the worst.

He recently asked me if we could get barbed wire around the fence in the garden. I wasn't surprised. His Christmas wish list the year before had been an iPad, some barbed wire and a Taser.

'Why do you want barbed wire on the fence?' I asked.

He replied, in a cheerful voice, 'A fox has attacked a baby. I saw it on the TV. We need to get barbed wire around the garden so it can't get in. We need to protect me and Jessi and Lily.'

There was no mention of the rest of the family . . .

CHAPTER 10

SOLDIERING ON

For Lorcan's eighth birthday in September 2012 we went to visit the historic town of Chester. We decided to go by train, to give the boys a different view of the journey from the usual bolt along the motorway, and it gives them more room to move about so they get less bored. Both boys love museums and historic sites, so we went from place to place finding out about the Romans. The weather was kind to us and we managed an ice cream sitting on a bench near the river.

Eventually, we ended up in the Grosvenor Museum, where the lady on the reception desk spotted the boys and told us that if we were quick we could see a demonstration involving Roman swords. With Lorcan's soldier obsession, it couldn't have been better, so we went to take a look.

In a large room in the museum, the guide stood next to a table that was covered in Roman weaponry. He gave a little speech and explained all about the weapons and armour, and he was great with the boys. Luke tried on some of the armour and was big enough to hold a real Roman sword, but Lorcan, being only eight, was given a wooden one to hold.

After the talk, we handed back the swords and I thanked the guide. We were just walking out when Lorcan, quick as a flash, grabbed a big metal sword from the table and thrust it forwards into an imaginary opponent. He was so fast the man didn't have time to stop him, but went pale before wrestling it off Lorcan. When we'd finally got it back, he told me it was thought to be the oldest sword on the table and was definitely not for general handling. He said he'd done plenty of demonstrations before, with lots of children, but he had never encountered one as quick as Lorcan!

We also went in the Dewa Roman Experience, which has a realistic Roman fortress complete with streets, barracks, a bathhouse, a taverna and market stalls. The boys loved this and they also got to go inside a reconstruction of a ship's galley, with a Roman oarsmaster guiding them through their 'journey'. There were helmets and armour for the children to try on, which was very exciting.

Going round museums with Lorcan is an experience. He moves very fast through the exhibits and tends to home in on things of particular interest to him. And he always insists on buying a sword in the gift shop – he's got quite a collection at home.

Lorcan loves to pretend he is historical characters. He recently spent several days during half-term dressed as Dick Turpin, complete with mask and hat. He declared his intention to be a highwayman when he grows up, before watching the Dick Turpin *Horrible Histories* video on YouTube over and over again. I now know the song by heart! He was also popping up in front of us all day yelling, 'Stand and deliver!'

One morning, he was up at five dressed as Dick Turpin and demanding that someone go downstairs with him for breakfast as he was scared – despite being a fierce highwayman. Throughout this game Jess was his faithful horse, whom he called Black Bethel because he didn't like the name Bess.

Birthdays tend to be a family event in our household. We usually get a cake and spend the day with family at my mum's, but we'll also have a day out, even if it is just a trip to the Imperial War Museum North, which is very close to home.

On one occasion, when Dave took the boys to the Imperial War Museum, they were stopped on the way and a man asked them to do a survey. It was about home gadgets and apps, and he was asking things such as 'Does anyone own an iPad?'

One of the questions was, 'How many apps have you downloaded and paid for this year?' Luke answered, 'Two. I got them for my birthday.' Suddenly, to Dave's surprise, Lorcan blurted out 'Seventy-three!' in a really loud voice.

Even Jess gets a little birthday celebration, with Lorcan playing master of ceremonies, of course. For her second birthday, in June 2012, we all gathered at my mum's and Jess was showered with gifts and passed round for cuddles. She got some lovely fluffy mice, which she likes to carry around with her and hide behind the settee. As she has no opposable thumbs, Lorcan volunteered to open her presents for her and showed her each new toy with delight. He also insisted we all sing 'Happy Birthday', even though he stood grinning and didn't join in. Jess was distinctly underwhelmed by the whole thing.

For Lorcan, quiet birthdays are often better, as parties can throw up all sorts of challenges. As well as unfamiliar people, there can be social situations he just doesn't understand.

In January, he attended a goodbye party for Ella, the little girl who helped him so much in nursery. She was moving to Australia, which was a shame, because she and Lorcan got on so well. At the end of the party, I watched two little girls as they both deliberately kicked Lorcan. It wasn't hard and not apparently malicious, so I didn't intervene, but I asked him about it later and he insisted it was OK.

'It was just a kick goodbye!' he said, quite emphatically.

The girls had told him this was an affectionate way of saying goodbye and he believed them. I

164

had to explain that it is wrong to kick – for whatever reason. It left me wondering what else could be going on that Lorcan thinks is perfectly acceptable behaviour. This is what is hard to get over.

He's good at school, he's well behaved, he does his work, he's a happy little thing. But what's going on that I don't know about? Often, children with Asperger's find it difficult to interpret people's intentions and, as he gets older, this could cause problems at school.

A month later the tickets to the 2013 Valentine's disco went on sale. It was after school, so not compulsory, and it's just a bit of fun. Lorcan had been to the Christmas discos and enjoyed them, so I asked him if I should get him a ticket.

'I'm not going!' he insisted.

'Why not?' I asked. 'I thought you liked the school disco.'

'Because you have to kiss girls!' he replied, his voice dripping with disgust.

I tried to explain that he didn't have to kiss anyone and it was just a lovely occasion to have fun with his friends, but he still refused to go. Someone had obviously told him that was the case and he wasn't taking the risk.

In December 2012, I noticed Cats Protection were holding a fundraising stall in the Pets at Home store, close to our home. I contacted them and offered to bring Jess in to see them and they were delighted with the idea and even had some posters made. I put Jess in her carrier and took her along, with Lorcan. I had bought a cat harness to use so we could put her on a lead, as I know dogs are allowed in Pets at Home and I needed some control over Jess, so she didn't scarper. She had never been on a harness before but she was great.

She wandered around the store exploring, sniffing the products and enjoying herself. Lorcan enjoyed walking her but, at one point, she wandered into a big dog kennel and got a bit tangled, so I had to help him get her out. Of course, he found it hilariously funny and announced, 'Jessi's pretending to be a dog!'

A few minutes later, he set off outside with her and sped off towards the next shop, so I had to take over the lead-holding duties.

Jess enjoyed being fussed over and happily submitted to being cuddled by the Cats Protection volunteers and strangers, who all thought she was gorgeous.

In March, eight months after Jess won the award, I was contacted by the producer of Jeremy Vine's BBC Radio 2 Show. He had seen the *Breakfast* piece while he was researching a show on selective-mutism awareness, so he wanted me to go on.

Once again, it was to be at MediaCityUK, but this time in a different building. Unfortunately, when I got there for the interview, nobody knew anything about it. I had to wait while they rang around and eventually called the producer in London. I was taken into a small studio for the interview, where I had to wait about half an hour until my turn. It was stressful but it is so important to spread awareness that I couldn't refuse to do it. Afterwards I met Dave and we went for a nice calming lunch. I was getting used to doing the interviews but the nerves still kicked in!

Since our first appearance, and Lorcan's later diagnosis, I have also been doing some interviews on behalf of Hearts and Minds Challenge (heartsandmindschallenge.org), who raise money to help children with autism. My first was on Radio Manchester, a few weeks before the Jeremy Vine show, and it was to talk about having a child on the autism spectrum in mainstream school. Monique from Hearts and Minds Challenge was with me, so that made it a bit easier, and it went well. I have also done a few magazine interviews, including one for a magazine that goes out to seven thousand primary schools. Again, that was on

Asperger's in mainstream education, but I also mentioned the selective mutism.

The awards have given me a platform to raise awareness of both conditions and we have Jess to thank, yet again, for that.

Lorcan's selective mutism presents problems that most parents will never have to think about. An eye test, for example, is pretty difficult if a child can't say, out loud, the letters he is reading on the chart.

On a recent trip to the optician's, Lorcan was completely silent throughout, not even a giggle. He sat in the chair and the optometrist asked if he was comfortable. He shook his head, solemnly. As it happens, though, the optometrist had heard the selective-mutism interview on the Jeremy Vine radio show, and understood the problem. He was fabulous and got through the test by getting Lorcan to draw the letters in the air with his fingers. He told me this was the first time he'd ever encountered a child with selective mutism.

The optometrist tested Lorcan's eyes really thoroughly and decided he would benefit from wearing glasses for schoolwork. Lorcan was not impressed, and shook his head emphatically when asked if he was pleased. Fortunately, he had come round to the idea by the time the glasses were ready and he has been wearing them in class and puts them safely in their case when he is not wearing them.

Lorcan's latest dental check-up, was a riot, too. He wanted Luke to be seen first but when it was Lorcan's turn he bounded up and leaped onto the chair, smiling widely. While his teeth were being checked his feet were constantly jiggling about, obviously a sign of nerves. At one point, the dentist mentioned that Lorcan would likely need a brace when he is older. Lorcan threw himself dramatically back on the chair, lay face down and then showed us a very comical 'devastated' face.

When he had finished, the dentist lowered the chair and Lorcan jiggled his way down the seat and climbed off right at the bottom, wriggling under the wires and equipment. He did it too quickly to be stopped. Lorcan never said a word from entering the dentist's until we were nearly at the car, but visits to the dentist have always been very strange. As a toddler he attended with Luke but would never open his mouth to let the dentist see his teeth. On one occasion, when he was two, he screamed really loudly when we tried to sit him on the chair and the dentist managed to sneak a look as he yelled.

The first time he willingly opened his mouth for the dentist, when he was five, was a huge shock.

He refused to sit on the chair but stood in the middle of the room and opened up as wide as he could, but he was obviously very anxious. All the time his mouth was open, he was letting out a strange, long, high-pitched squeal.

Since then he has agreed to sit on the chair and open his mouth, but he has never spoken.

To the dentist and optician I have time to explain Lorcan's silence, but others may well think he's just impolite. He can now talk in front of strangers, which to me is a huge step forward, but it can make his inability to talk *to* them look even worse. We recently booked a family holiday and, as we sat in the travel agent's, he was chatting away to us in front of the lady taking our booking but, when she asked him a direct question, he just ignored her. When they're little, nobody is offended by that and it's OK, but there is going to come a point where people will start to think, What a rude child!

In May, I took Lily to the vet's for her annual booster. When we got back I thought that it seemed a long time since Jess had been in, so I dug out her vaccination card and saw that she had been due in March. I rang the vet for an appointment and was told that the last time she had a jab was in 2011. I booked an appointment but assumed there was some mistake, so I got out her card to check and they were right: she hadn't been done at all during 2012. During that time, I'd taken her to MediaCityUK, to school and on a lead to the Pets at Home fundraising with Cats Protection. I was horrified.

She went for the immunization along with Lily, who needed to see the vet as well, and Lorcan came along to keep her company. Lily was seen first, while Jess stayed in her box. Lorcan was messing about, looking at things and fiddling with things, opening and shutting the door repeatedly so I sent him out to wait in the waiting room with my mum.

Jess was terrified when she had to be examined. She went all floppy and meek with her ears back and she was quiet. She was very well behaved but clearly didn't like being messed about with and she seemed very relieved to go back in her little box afterwards.

On the way home, Lorcan was most concerned. He sat in the back of the car with her, constantly looking to see if she was OK, and asking, 'Are you OK, Jess? Did the needle hurt?'

In summer 2012, when we had a day or two of sunshine, I put Lorcan's tent up in the garden for the boys to play in. As I was pottering around the house I had a sudden panic as I noticed that the back door was open and Jess was nowhere to be seen. After yelling, 'The cat's got out!' at the top of my voice, I dashed out into the garden to start the search. I was rushing round the garden calling Jessi's name when I suddenly heard a little voice coming from the tent. It was Lorcan saying, 'No, Jessi, you have to be a good captive and

171

remain in this prison.' He'd zipped her in the tent to play a game of pirates without telling me. And I'm sure she was enjoying every minute.

I'm glad that when we received the official letter with the Asperger's diagnosis, they also wrote that Lorcan still has selective mutism. Although he is speaking very well in school, where he now feels more comfortable and relaxed, he is often selectively mute elsewhere, in less familiar situations. That is why I believe he will regress when he leaves the comfort of primary school to go to the larger and altogether more frightening environment of a secondary. This will need to be carefully managed by us and his future teachers. He has made fantastic progress but he is by no means over the SM.

My worries about Lorcan's secondary school came out recently in a Facebook chat with a friend of mine. Christine McLaughlin's a teacher, trained in special educational needs, who runs a local tuition centre called Better Tuition (bettertuition. co.uk). She has always been very supportive of our family. One day I was moaning about my secondary-school dilemma and she asked me what I would like to happen, in an ideal world. I said I'd like a special unit in a local school for children like

Lorcan whose needs tend to be overlooked, as they often seem to cope at school until their teenage years.

'What is the chance, do you think, of my persuading a school to set up a special unit for children with Asperger's syndrome?' I asked.

She replied, 'Well, I suppose it would be a question of funding, but it definitely is needed.' She mentioned a similar unit in Sale, near Manchester, and suggested I ring the Special Educational Needs Coordinator – or SENCo – there for a chat.

Then she added, 'Of course, you could look into alternative education – like forest schools, or set up your own thing, a part-time group or flexi-school Lorcan to fit in with it? I could help you with that – and you could use my premises.' (Forest schools are outdoor-education organizations that allow people to learn social and technical skills in a woodland setting.)

That idea of a support group really got me thinking. A while ago, I'd spoken with another friend who has a son on the autistic spectrum and we had discussed setting up such a group. It proved more difficult than we had anticipated and our plans had come to nothing, but, now that Christine was on board and offering us use of her business premises, it began to look like a possibility.

We started by putting together some ideas. We decided we needed two aspects to the group. The first would be for young children like Lorcan, to ensure they get the early intervention that the experts say is crucial. We want the little ones to learn social skills, communication skills and all the things children with Asperger's are missing. Second, we felt it was very important to have something for the older children and young adults. Research has shown that depression is a major problem for people on the autistic spectrum, so a group where they can meet and not feel isolated would be a huge step forward.

We decided to hold an open meeting, and got the ball rolling by emailing around and putting a poster on Twitter and Facebook. Crucially, we specified that diagnosis was not required, as many children spend years going through diagnosis, and many others, like my son Adam, are not diagnosed until later in their teens. We wanted to help anyone with a child on the higher-functioning end of the spectrum or with the social skills deficiency.

Too many children, like Lorcan, have been given a diagnosis and not offered the professional help they need. Nobody knows better than I do what can happen if help is not offered, but I'm quite an assertive person and am capable of fighting for my son. There are other parents who would not know where to turn. We want to be able to help them.

That week I attended a Fairtrade coffee morning at the constituency offices of our local Member of Parliament, Kate Green. I mentioned the group to her and she was really interested. After listening to our ideas she said she would help as necessary and endorse the project. We are so lucky to have such a supportive MP.

As luck would have it, across the room I spotted George Devlin, a local campaigner who has a lot of involvement in community issues. I mentioned the idea to George, who also offered to be involved, and we soon had offers of support from many local councillors, including Councillor Joanne Harding, who joined our little committee.

With the momentum gathering, I emailed Trafford Council to tell them of our plans and had a very encouraging meeting with them at Easter. I also met with Ian McGrath, director of the Hearts and Minds Challenge charity, who offered us training at a future date.

The first meeting was held at Christine's tuition business. We had made no specific plans and had no idea how many would turn up, and the evening turned into a bit of scrum. A seemingly endless stream of parents filed in and we soon ran out of chairs. Adam had been drafted in to take notes, but space was so tight that both he and Christine had to sit outside the room. Councillor Harding arrived but couldn't get a seat so had to leave.

We had parents of children from Lorcan's age through all the school years right up to teenagers. All the stories were similar: struggling with the system, not getting enough help. Many of the teens and older, several of whom were at grammar school, were depressed and failing at school despite doing well with GCSEs. We all had a good chat, established there was most definitely a need for our group and arranged to meet up a month later.

The next meeting was another full house. Fortunately (in a way), at least eight people from the first meeting couldn't make it, but we had one or two new faces as well. We shared ideas again. George Devlin announced he had applied for some funding for us and we had a representative from the National Autistic Society befriending team, who spoke to the group.

The spirit of sharing and cooperation was truly uplifting. One grandparent offered her services as a babysitter, and a parent, who is a hypnotherapist, offered to teach relaxation techniques to the group.

Moving forward, some of us plan to undertake training so we can help our children ourselves. I'm also keen for Adam to get involved with the support group for teens. He has experienced the issues himself and has lots of experience to share.

Amazingly, after starting the group, I found out that Trafford actually has an adult autism coordinator. Considering that Adam has been a Trafford resident all his life and was diagnosed six years ago, it's remarkable we were never told about this.

We met with her and she listed all the things she can do in her role for over-eighteens. It was infuriating, as everything she listed I want for Lorcan, too: help with social skills, communication skills, assertiveness. Why not teach these things to children as well as adults?

The group are now – at the time of writing – on

the verge of organizing daytime meetings, as we have some parents who have childcare issues, so can't make the evening meetings, and we are getting a good team together. We are sending out a monthly email to our families and support is growing all the time. It feels good to do something positive about the challenges faced by families of autistic children.

Lorcan is a real giggler. He recently came home from school and told me, 'I think I've lost my sense of humour. I couldn't laugh at school. Nothing was funny.' But, with his ready smile and his sense of mischief, I don't think that's ever going to happen. He even giggles when he's in trouble.

Lorcan is frequently being told off for fighting with Luke. The last time I gave him a bit of a scolding, he smiled sweetly and batted his eyelashes at me, to try to put me off.

'Is that what you do at school when you're in trouble?' I asked. 'Does it work on the teachers?'

'I'm good at school,' he answered. 'I don't get told off. You just tell me off for the wrong reasons.' By this time he was laughing hysterically, but he managed to add, 'I shouldn't be told off for fighting. I have to protect myself and defend myself.' It's hard to stay cross, sometimes.

On another occasion he was harassing Lily, so I said, 'Lorcan, leave the dog alone. Do you want me to find you something to do?'

Lorcan replied, chuckling. 'No, no, no – Miss Trunchbull!' He then spent the afternoon lobbing water balloons over the garden fence while I wasn't looking, and then sneaked into next door's garden to pinch their wooden mallet, which he brought back to our house.

Jess can always bring out his sense of humour too. She has now taken to creeping into Lorcan's bedroom when he goes to bed and, after spending some time looking out of the window and trampling on his toys, she jumps on the bed and crawls under the covers. It's not ideal when we're trying to get him to sleep, since her tail tickles him and makes him giggle and her bedtime antics send him into helpless laughter.

He is very protective of her as well – and that wild imagination sees danger for her at every turn. He has come dashing downstairs shouting, 'We need help! Quick! Jessi's sniffing the lava lamp and you said not to touch it. It's dangerous! Save Jessi!' The daft cat was curled around the lava lamp in his bedroom and when I removed her Lorcan made a huge fuss of her.

'Are you OK, Jessi?' he said. 'That was very dangerous indeed, wasn't it?'

Unlike many cats, Jess actually loves water and

sits on the side of the bath when Lorcan is in it. But, if she tries to clean herself, he tells her, 'Don't lick yourself Jessi, it's unhygienic!'

In March 2013, Lorcan was finally invested into the Cubs. He had moved up from Beavers some months earlier but had found the change stressful, despite enjoying it once he was actually there. Luke had moved up to Scouts at the same time but the leaders suggested he go with Lorcan for the first few weeks, so the poor lad had to do both Cubs and Scouts for months. I did give him a bit of extra pocket money to make it worth his while.

On the night Lorcan was finally settled enough to be invested, I knew he would have to say the Cub Promise out loud and I was nervous for him. We were invited to go and watch Lorcan and I was so wound up about what would happen that I forgot my camera. We arrived a few minutes before the end of the session and were shown to seats. The Scouts, including Luke, were standing in a circle, doing their official Scout sign-off and saying promises. Normally, we don't get to see this as we all wait outside until the sessions are over, so it was encouraging to see Lorcan saluting and joining in.

When the usual stuff was done the boys who were being invested were led up to the Akela (the Cubs' adult leader) by an older Scout and Lorcan went up with his friend George. Both boys had the Cub Scout promise written down in case they had forgotten it. Lorcan and George said the promise together and we could actually hear Lorcan's voice, loud and clear. It was the first time ever in such a situation, so we were really proud.

George's mum kindly took a photo of the boys. We congratulated Lorcan but we made sure we didn't make a big fuss, as I want him to feel that speaking in these circumstances is normal. When we got home Jessi was waiting at the door and Lorcan got straight down on the floor to tell her his news.

'Guess what, Jessi. I'm a Cub Scout now!' he announced. 'I've been invested – whatever that means!'

When Lorcan first moved up we got a letter about a Cub camp in May. Lorcan was adamant he wasn't going, and I was not surprised, as he spends most nights in Luke's room and has never been away for the night without one of us. In the end, they decided to camp for one night at the Scout HQ, where they go for the Cub meeting every week. When I told him, Lorcan initially said he wanted to go, which was great, but I wasn't entirely convinced.

A little while later he mentioned it and said he wasn't going, but I ignored it, as the camp was weeks away and I thought he might change his mind again. As the date drew nearer, the children were all talking about the camp and Lorcan seemed really keen. On the final Cubs session before camp, I went in and had words with the leaders and they assured me that he would be in a tent with his friends from school, and that they would phone if any problems.

On the night of the camp, I had tickets to attend the Mayor's Ball, so I was still a bit worried about Lorcan going, but I thought it would be good for him. Luke was able to prepare Lorcan, as he is a seasoned Scout and has camped lots of times. On the day, we packed his sleeping bag, pyjamas and toothbrush and he insisted on packing two torches – 'just in case'. When we dropped him off in the afternoon, we noticed the tents in the grounds, some modern, some old-fashioned with tent pegs. Lorcan was reading the first Famous Five book at the time, so I pointed out that the older tents were the sort the Famous Five would have slept in.

We took him to sign in and left him with his friends. He had an anxious face when we left, but was happy to stay. I knew he would be fine with his friends and he would enjoy the camp. It was also good for him to sleep away from home occasionally, as he would need to go on the school residential trip in Year Five.

I went off to the ball leaving Dave with his phone switched on in case of disaster.

The next morning at ten o'clock we picked him up and, to our relief, he was fine. They had made a camp fire and cooked breakfast on it, and Lorcan told me they'd been up until around one in the morning messing about. They had certainly kept the leaders busy.

Lorcan had enjoyed himself, but was very glad to be home again. He gave poor Lily a hearty slap on her bottom and cuddled Jess as soon as he got in. He was in a good mood that day, despite being tired, so I knew that he had enjoyed himself. Hopefully, the next time a longer camp comes up, he will feel up to going.

A month after Lorcan's investment came an even bigger test of his confidence. His class had been learning about the Romans – one of his favourite subjects – and they had arranged their class assembly around it. They were to do a little play and Lorcan, who was playing a Roman soldier, had a few lines to learn. He studied them hard and practised and, as the day of the play approached, I watched carefully for signs of anxiety. The usual giveaway is not sleeping and getting irritable but neither of those seemed to be evident. He knew his lines off by heart and seemed really pleased with himself.

A few days before, I asked him if he was nervous about the play.

'No, I am not,' he said firmly. 'I'm really excited about my class play.'

As Lorcan didn't know what he was wearing, we popped into school and asked his teacher if he needed costumes and props. Mrs Bernard said he would need a white sheet, so it could be made into a toga, and mentioned that the class were short of swords. That was one area in which we could definitely help out! As I said earlier, Lorcan has a collection of swords of all descriptions at home, so I offered to bring some in and Lorcan agreed. I was really pleased because Lorcan has always been reluctant to bring things into school before, in case they get damaged or lost.

We rushed home and Lorcan sorted through the swords, which ranged from pirate cutlasses to Harry Potter's Gryffindor model. He carefully selected the suitable ones and we took them in.

The night before the play Lorcan went to bed as usual. I sneaked in to check on him about half an hour later, half expecting him to be wide awake and worrying. He was fast asleep.

The next morning he was up bright and early. He was singing on the way to school – something from Minecraft, one of his favourite games – and he was smiling as I waved him off. Before I left the playground, Lorcan's teacher, Mrs Bernard, came to have a quick word.

'He's been saying his lines in rehearsal all week,'

she told me. 'But I'm not sure what'll happen when he has a proper audience.'

After that, I had a restless morning, wondering how he would get on. The class have done lots of plays but Lorcan has always had a nonspeaking part, so this was going to be interesting. As I was setting off, my mum rang and asked if she could come and watch, too, so we arrived together. We were really early as I wanted a front-row seat, but the chairs at the back of the hall soon filled up with parents and grandparents and, eventually, the whole school filed in along with all the staff. Then Year Three took their places on the stage, and Mrs O'Connor, the head teacher, introduced the class, and the play started.

Lorcan stood on the stage and kept grinning at us. I had my camcorder at the ready as Lorcan had insisted I film him when he stood up and walked to the middle of the stage, so I was on tenterhooks the whole time. I must confess, in my anxious state, I didn't hear a word of the play.

At last the big moment arrived. He suddenly stood up and walked to the front with another boy. I switched the camcorder on and waited. The other boy spoke, then it was Lorcan's turn. I held my breath to calm the butterflies in my tummy as he went to open his mouth. Then he delivered his lines, really clearly and beautifully.

Tears sprang to my eyes but I stopped myself from crying, and smiled at him. He looked absolutely fine, just a little bit fidgety, and his hands went to his mouth when he sat down, but he'd done it!

Later in the play, he had another sentence to say but it went too quickly for me to film it. He delivered that perfectly, too.

After the final bow, the head teacher and Lorcan's Reception teacher, Mrs Mellor, came over to talk to me. Mrs Mellor admitted to a few tears of her own and Mrs O'Connor said the staff had actually gasped when Lorcan delivered his lines. Mrs Bernard looked overjoyed. A lot of the parents, who knew about Lorcan's selective mutism, also congratulated us, which was wonderful.

When we got home Lorcan was as high as a kite, singing away to himself. After he'd played on his iPad for a while we put the video on and he sat smiling happily as he watched himself.

David and I couldn't believe he had stood up on stage, in front of a packed school hall, and spoken out loud. It was a huge achievement for Lorcan and one that, pre-Jess, would have been beyond our wildest dreams. I couldn't have been prouder.

EPILOGUE

ABOUT A BOY

In her letter to the *Birman Cat Club Magazine*, after Jessi-cat had scooped the Cat of the Year award, her breeder Janet Bowen, wrote: 'Birmans truly have a soul and seem to know what is required of them.'

On the friendship between Lorcan and Jess, she added, 'These two soulmates were meant to be together . . . if a Birman is truly loved they give back more than you will ever need.' I couldn't agree more.

Jess is gentle and nonjudgemental and seems to sense that Lorcan really needs her. She makes a beeline for him above other members of the family, although she loves us all, and he adores her company. She is there to greet him when he gets home and is by his side most of the time that he's there. Even when she's not with him the impact she has had on every aspect of his life, and especially his school work, is clear. She constantly makes him smile and she gives him confidence. Because of Jess, Lorcan is making real progress in dealing with his selective mutism, speaking to teachers, to most of his classmates and even to unfamiliar adults.

But perhaps the most amazing thing is that she

186

has taught him how to express his emotions – and to say, 'I love you.'

Lorcan's school has recently invested in lots of resources aimed at children on the autistic spectrum, and is implementing regular sessions to deal with and talk about emotions. This is a necessary tool for both social development and furthering their education. Lorcan himself seems to have only the extremes, so he's either very happy and smiley or devastated and crying. Other emotions, such as love and affection, are hard for him to identify with and, before Jess came along, I'm sure he had no idea how they felt or how to articulate them.

We have never doubted that Lorcan loves us, but at times it has been tough.

This is a little lad who hated cuddles, didn't like to be touched and couldn't express affection in the conventional way – even towards his mum and dad. Heartbreaking though that was for us, we were lucky, because we always knew, deep down, that he had Asperger's syndrome or some form of autism and that it wasn't our fault.

Then along came Jess – our Bluegenes Angel – with her big blue eyes, soft fluffy fur and endless patience.

Jess has taught Lorcan to hug and kiss, to care about someone else, and to put her needs before his own. It's a hugely important lesson. Children on the autistic spectrum often struggle with empathy, but Lorcan most definitely empathizes with Jess and, in time, that may well teach him to empathize with people, too.

Since he was small, Lorcan has struggled to tell us if something is worrying him, upsetting him or causing anxiety. He wouldn't even tell us if he'd had a bad day. As selective mutism is an anxiety disorder, not a speech problem, that makes it doubly difficult to tackle the root cause of the problem.

To hear him babbling away to Jess about his day at school, about the good and the bad, as she sits wide-eyed and intent, twitching her ears in response, is music to our ears. She answers his chatter with loud miaows and loving head rubs, and the discourse between them is as close to a proper conversation I have ever seen between a child and a pet.

Three years ago, when Jess came into our home, it was almost as if Lorcan were two different people: a happy, chatty boy at home but struck dumb by crippling anxiety at school. Today, he can stand up in front of the class to talk about his pet, can say his Scout promise out loud, read to his teachers and can even take part in the school play. To Dave and me, and all who love him, that is nothing short of a minor miracle.

They say a dog is a man's best friend, but for our little boy Jessi-cat is more than a best friend – she's a lifeline. Thanks to her, Lorcan has a brighter future ahead of him and his faithful cat companion will be with him, every step of the way.

This friendly, curious, playful and beautiful bundle of fur has broken the silence and enabled our son to finally find his voice.

FAME FOR JESSI-CAT
AND LORCAN

The following is taken from an article written for the *Birman Cat Club Magazine*, Issue 75, Winter 2012.

The Birman who Transformed the Life of a Boy with a Severe Anxiety Disorder

by Adam Preston

This August, my little brother, Lorcan, and his cat, Jessi-cat, attended the Cats Protection National Cat Awards 2012 at the Savoy Hotel in London. Jessi-cat was a finalist in the Best Friends category, having gained world-wide recognition since her nomination, due to her incredible relationship with Lorcan. This is what happened.

In May of this year, my mum Jayne (Dillon) saw a post on Twitter, requesting stories of exceptional cats who have in some way helped their owner overcome obstacles or improve their quality of life. Lorcan's friendship with our two-year-old Birman,

Jessi-cat, immediately came to mind, and we responded to their appeal.

Lorcan is in many ways similar to every other eight-year-old boy; he enjoys playing with his toy soldiers and playing football with his other brother, Luke. However, Lorcan has selective mutism, an anxiety disorder which means he finds it difficult – or often impossible – to speak in particular situations. Someone with selective mutism, although capable of speech and able to understand language, won't speak under certain circumstances or in front of specific people (often strangers or adults, and sometimes even members of their own family), yet may be extremely talkative and outgoing at home. Although they may also be shy or suffer from social anxiety, selective mutism itself is not the same as shyness.

In children, the disorder often becomes apparent when they start school. While many children are initially reluctant to speak upon entering a new environment, children with selective mutism won't eventually 'come out of their shell' as is expected. Their inability to speak to their teachers and classmates becomes clear as their silence continues. Unfortunately, because of the nature of the condition, children with selective mutism are often overlooked and do not receive the help they need. They may be perceived as simply 'quiet' or even stubborn, refusing to talk. As they are not disruptive or troublesome at school, many of them will therefore not receive any assistance. And this is where Jessi-cat comes in!

There's plenty of evidence to show the huge benefits of therapy animals and pets, particularly for children and especially those with communication or speech problems, such as autism or selective mutism. Although we were aware of this when we brought home Jessi-cat in 2010, little did we know just how much she would help to change Lorcan's life.

Jessi-cat is a beautiful blue Birman with brilliant blue eyes and an extremely fluffy tail. She was bred by Janet Bowen in Lancashire and her pedigree name is Bluegenes Angel. She's very vocal, often maintaining a conversation with other members of the family and greeting us when we approach her. Being incredibly friendly and curious, Jessi-cat is always interested in what Lorcan is up to. She'll watch him playing with his toys and often joins in the game herself.

Within days of Jessi-cat's nomination being announced, Granada Television were in touch to find out more, and Lorcan and Jessi-cat were featured on the local news. This was only the start of their fame, as Jessi-cat's story spread to national newspapers, animal publications, numerous foreign-language websites and even TV shows. We've just recently found out she's to appear in a Spanish book!

When the day of the awards ceremony arrived, Lorcan travelled down to London with our mum Jayne (Jessi-cat wasn't able to make the journey), eager to find out if his furry friend had won the prestigious award. They went straight to the Savoy Hotel, where lunch was served before the award ceremony itself began. When the Best Friends category was introduced first, Jessi-cat was announced as the winner (her photo eliciting many expressions of 'Aww' throughout the room), but the main award was yet to come.

Lorcan later said he kept his fingers crossed all through the ceremony, and his wish was granted when the chief executive of Cats Protection revealed that the overall winner and Cat of the Year 2012 was indeed Jessi-cat! Jessi-cat's popularity was reflected in the huge cheer which erupted when she was announced as overall winner. An elated Lorcan walked confidently up to the front of the room to collect the award with a beaming smile on his face. He even lifted the award above his head as the official photographer snapped away in front of him.

Lorcan and my mum were presented with a bouquet of flowers, cat-related gifts and a cat mask. While at the ceremony, they were also able to meet the creator of the famous cartoon, *Simon's Cat*, Simon Tofield, winner of the Celebrity Cat category, who even drew a lovely picture for Lorcan to take home. Before leaving, there were interviews to give and photos to be taken, and

Lorcan arrived home very excited after his day at the National Cat Awards. He was delighted for his little friend, who welcomed him home with lots of miaows and head-rubs.

The next morning, Lorcan, with Mum and Luke, took Jessi-cat to the BBC studios for an interview with Radio 5 Live and the morning TV programme, *Breakfast*. She behaved impeccably and even had free run of the green room before entering the studio. The reaction from viewers showed just how appealing she is to others, with the video of her *Breakfast* appearance proving immensely popular online.

For winning both the Best Friends category and Cat of the Year, Jessi-cat won a year's supply of cat litter, three months' worth of cat food, a framed photo of herself and two trophies with her name on them. Since becoming an international celebrity, Jessi-cat has been the focus of much attention: her story has been covered by countless news websites and magazines across the world and she has loved every minute of it, posing and peering appealingly into the cameras of surprised photographers. The official Cats Protection video of Jessi-cat has received over 130,000 views so far on YouTube!

Lorcan has made lots of improvement over the last two years, and much of that has been down to his friendship and close bond with Jessi-cat. They became inseparable and he's able to show affection towards her and express love for her in ways he can't do with anyone else. As Mum said in a press interview: 'She's such a delightful responsive cat and he hugs and kisses her all the time . . . She is without a doubt the best friend a boy could have and has had a huge positive impact on his life.' Lorcan is now able to say 'I love you' for the first time, and he's started communicating with people he doesn't know very well and even reads to one of the teachers now – something he's never done before. And combined with the support he's receiving from his school and teachers, Jessi-cat's comfort and companionship are finally helping him find his voice.

Cats Protection are overjoyed with the awareness Lorcan and Jessi-cat have raised about cats and their often-overlooked qualities as pets. With the help he's receiving from his school and at home, Lorcan is making huge improvements and showing that, with the right help, children with selective mutism can excel and even overcome their anxiety eventually. Jessi-cat shows just how much a cat can change a person's life, no matter how old they are!

*The sketch Simon Tofield kindly drew for Lorcan at the Cats
Protection National Cat of the Year Awards.*